Leon

A Lost Childhood

Leon Henderson

authorHOUSE®

AuthorHouse™ UK Ltd.
500 Avebury Boulevard
Central Milton Keynes, MK9 2BE
www.authorhouse.co.uk
Phone: 08001974150

First published by AuthorHouse 6/11/2009

ISBN: 978-1-4389-8672-2 (sc)

This book is printed on acid-free paper.

I dedicate this book to my soulmate Scraggy who has shown me the true meaning of love, my two beautiful children Levi & Dylan who light up my heart, my two precious sisters Nicola and Jacqui whom I love dearly, Jan and John who I love more than words could ever say. Thank you both for your undying faith in me, and for showing me the true meaning of the words 'mam' and 'dad'.

To my special Uncle Jim and Auntie Jacci who supported me at a time in my life when I needed it most, your kindness is never forgotten.

Grandad George, gone but not forgotten, gran, sandra and dear friends Danni, Donna, Elaine, Mark and Grant.

Steve Dolan who gave me the confidence to write this book, your skills in tutoring and friendship made this all possible.

Lastly, for anyone throughout my life, people who have come and gone, i hold you all in my memories. You have all changed my life in your own special and unique way.

I dragged my weary body upstairs, slowly, with that singular feeling of being the odd-one-out: that sense of complete and utter worthlessness.

Would they even notice if I were dead?

Probably not.

I entered my bedroom where, staring at me, was my best friend, Orville, the green duck I was given on the same Christmas I was told there was no Santa Claus. It wasn't said in nastiness. Enid had tried hard to find me an Orville, but, as they were so popular, there was a frenzy to buy them that year and I think she worried that I would think Santa had left me out. Orville had been my best friend ever since.

I'm going to go.

I'm going to run away, far, far away.

After all, it wouldn't be the first time that I had done it.

I was placed into a children's home in the summer holidays of '87 because, apparently, Enid and Jim wouldn't have been able to cope with Beverly and me for the holidays.

It had seemed strange to me at the time, as I knew that I hadn't even been particularly badly-behaved in the lead-up to that decision; however, the real reason for sending me away only became clear many years later when the true horror of my sister's abuse unfolded.

I ran away from that children's home even though, ironically, it was there that I had wanted to stay; but the powers-that-be were determined I was returning to my foster parents after the holidays.

I had other ideas!

Until that point, I'd been afraid of children's homes, as the stories they had recanted had led me to believe that these homes were reminiscent of a setting from "Oliver Twist". All of which I soon came to appreciate to be false.

A girl and I hatched a plan to escape when she wanted to go to visit her boyfriend who lived in her hometown of Pendal, about 20 miles away from where we were living. Donna was 16 and seemed to have so much more life experience than me; I felt safe with her.

We climbed out of the first floor bedroom window and slithered down the drainpipe. It was pouring and we had to run across a field which was so muddy that my shoe stuck and then disappeared; so there we were, on hands and knees, searching for my missing shoe in a pitch-black, muddy field. Eventually, we found it and continued to walk all through the night.

However, just as daylight broke through, a police car appeared behind us and that was it!

We tried so hard to convince them that we weren't the kids for whom they were looking. Needless to say we failed and so it wasn't long before we were on our way back to the home, where we were taken into the office and made to feel like criminals. Mrs. Hunt went through both of us like the proverbial hurricane; then she asked Donna to leave as she wanted to speak to me alone.

It was then I learned that, the very evening I had chosen to run away, my grandfather had died unexpectedly. I couldn't believe it. My heart felt crushed. Why that night? Was it my punishment for running away? I promised God from that day on that I would never run away again.

Now, here I was, about to break that promise.

My heart was pumping the blood around my body at such a speed that I began to feel faint. Beads of sweat were trickling down my face.

What am I doing?

If I get caught for this, I'm dead meat. I'll be battered black and blue for a start but, worse than that, emotionally raped, again and again, until my head spins. That sickly feeling as my mouth goes dry and I feel as though I haven't eaten for days on end. Head pounding, heart racing, shaking and looking for an escape route in my mind where, if I dig deep enough, I reach that place where no-one can trap me or take away my sanity. This is a game to that evil bastard. He actually wants to destroy me. The hate I feel for him eats away at my sanity.

I can't let him win.

I won't let him win.

Without even thinking, I get dressed and put on my jacket.

I'll climb out of the window. Shit, I can't: Mary, from next door, is across the road talking to someone. If she sees me climbing out of the window she will be right over the road to tell all.

Sod it! I'll sneak out of the front door. I don't actually care anymore.

What can they do? They've already destroyed me. There's nothing to lose, when there's nothing left.

Quickly, I run down the stairs, right past the living-room door and into the hallway. This is it. Once I go out through that front door, it is the point of no return. I can't go back. I must make sure that Mary doesn't think anything suspicious is happening, otherwise my cover is blown. I close the front door quietly behind me. I've done it! Oh my God! Think,

think, and think quickly. The palms of my hands are sweating. I feel sick. God, please let me get away: Please help me escape this, once and for all.

"Hiya", I call to Mary as I pass her on the other side of the road. She lifts her head and smiles.

"I've done it", I whisper to myself, excitedly.

I need enough time to get to Anthony's house: he's my only friend, my only hope. I don't even know how far it is to Kensom. It must be at least 50 miles. As soon as Mary is out of sight, my walk quickly becomes a sprint.

Just keep going, keep running and don't stop to think.

I run for what seems like miles and miles. I don't have a watch, but it must be getting late, darkness is starting to fall all around me. "Shit" I curse myself. I didn't pick up matches for the cigarettes I'd nicked from their bedroom before I left. I really should have planned this. I've brought no extra clothes and I've got 20 Benson and Hedges, a £10 note and no matches.

I pass a sign for Raven-Hill. I must have run for four miles because that's how far it is to this point from Kirkby Willows; I only know this because my school bus turns down that road everyday. There's a row of houses on my right. I cross over the road. I'll knock at one of the doors and ask for some matches.

I can't even remember what I say to the man who answers, but I walk away with a new box of Swan matches. I light a cigarette. I've calmed down a little now.

I wonder if they've found out I'm missing yet?

I can't believe how far I've made it without being caught. I don't feel scared at all, for some reason. I am conscious of a really strong presence by my side. It's a strange, but very warm, secure feeling.

"We've done it!" I tell myself.

I've always been two people, for as long as I can remember: me and my thoughts chatting to each other, keeping each other safe and sane.

That's what Jim hated. I'm convinced he knew that I was aware of the fact that he was trying to destroy me: break my spirit, kill my soul.

Why did he hate me so much? Why try to destroy the mind of a 14 year old? What had I done that had been so bad that he hated every breath I drew into my pathetic, puny body? I only wanted him to be my dad, to look after me and protect me from all the boys at school who had bullied me for years and years at every single school I'd attended.

The humiliation of having a can of soda poured over your head on the school bus while everyone looks on and laughs, and being so gutless that you don't even fight back. The abuse continuing when you get off the bus to wait on the hillside for the connection: it arrives and the other kids witness you being degraded even further, as, having had horse shit thrown at you, it's now dripping down your face.

Boarding the bus to a wave of pointing and name-calling; why does everyone hate me so much?

Why does HE hate me so much?

I know why. Because he could tear me apart limb from limb, beat me black and blue, spit at me, kick me, drag me down flights of stairs by my ears, tell me that he knew I'd stolen money from his wallet and food from the pantry even though he knew - and I knew - I hadn't. But he could never, ever reach my other me.

My thoughts.

It's just those thoughts and me now: the thoughts that have kept me alive up to this point; the thoughts that have kept me going through all the psychological torture. I'm never going back there. I'll keep running.

How far have I got now? There hasn't been a signpost for ages. It's really dark now. I'll have another cigarette and then I'll start hitching for a lift.

"Is it thumb up or thumb down to stop a car?" I ask my other self.

"Shit, I can't remember," I answer. Just try both ways; someone is bound to stop, eventually. Car after car drives past me as though I don't exist. Wearing a black bomber jacket on a dark night doesn't really go in my favour though, does it! Every time another car approaches I feel a burst of excitement thinking that this might be the one that stops. I am aware of car headlights shining behind me.

This is the one.

I know it.

The car slows down.

"Oh my God, it's worked, we've done it!" we tell ourselves, pleased with the result. Then, suddenly, a barrage of questions starts to flood my thoughts. What if he's a murderer like the one in the film I'd seen recently?

Where do I say I'm going? Who am I going to see? What if he realizes that I've run away?

It's too late now; the car has come to a standstill. The passenger- side door swings open.

"Get in then," the guy behind the wheel says, in a kind voice.

My 'other' me has a strange thought.

Why do I feel all warm inside? Is it normal to have this warm feeling inside me? Immediately, I am hanging on to every word this man says. Is it, at last, my turn to receive some love?

What kind of love?

Will he touch me like they do on television?

I want him to do that, don't I?

I tell this guy I've missed the bus back to Kensom and that I need to make my way there.

"It's your lucky night then" he replies in his soft voice, "I'm going through Kensom, so I can drop you off there".

I drift off in the warmth from the car heater. All I can really remember is creating a scenario in my head in which this man kidnaps me and keeps me for himself, doing whatever he wants to me. After all, that's all I want.

To be wanted.

The words wake me up, wake me up and flood my subconscious.

"Wake up, you're here. Wake up" I hear the unfamiliar, yet kind voice. I sit bolt upright. Where am I? What time is it?

"Hey, it's o.k. You fell asleep, so I thought I would just leave you in peace," said the guy driving the car.

"I'm here? Thank you, thank you so much," I reply as I get out of the car and close the door behind me.

I start walking up a steep hill, block after block of grey buildings surrounding me. This is the way to Anthony's home as far as I can remember; it looks somewhat familiar. I remember Anthony taking me to old Millie's house; hers is the one with the red light on. Anthony says she's a prostitute and has been for as long as he can remember. Men go past her house and, if the red light is shining, it means she's free for sex. I knew all about prostitutes after seeing the series *Band of Gold*, about prostitutes who were murdered one by one and you weren't able to guess who it had been right up to the very end.

I loved that show.

It's really dark now. I'm not hungry. Strange! I thought I would be. I hope Anthony lets me stay tonight. I haven't even thought about what I'll do tomorrow.

Maybe his mum will let me live there with them. He's allowed to smoke AND he can stay up and watch *Prisoner Cell Block H.*

I had stayed at Anthony's house once before when I told him to ask his mum to phone Enid and convince her to let me have a sleepover one night after school. They were going on another fancy foreign break, without Beverly and me, so it didn't take much persuasion for her to say yes. It was only ever 'yes' if it was convenient for them; if it wasn't, then the answer would always be:

"No, you can't be trusted"

I'd heard that line so many times. One occasion, I remember in particular.

It was the first year of my new secondary school and I so desperately wanted to fit in. (This was before the horse shit incident.)

The school disco was being held one Friday and I'd never been to a school disco before.

"Can I go to the school disco on Friday?" I asked, although knowing already that the bitch would say no.

"No, you can't be trusted" she snapped back, without even bothering to consider it. I hated them so much. Why were they so strict?

That night, the home telephone rang. Enid answered, "77146 ..... Who?...

…What for? …Right," she muttered. " It's for you," she growled at me, her eyes burning through my head. I looked round and there he was as well, Jim, glaring at me with those accusing looks as if to say, "I'm watching you".

"Hello," I said nervously into the mouthpiece. It was Claire, from my class at school, asking if I would go to the school disco on Friday. I desperately wanted to go, to prove I was normal. This was my chance to start a new school with real friends. She had said that she was going to call and she had. I grew excited inside my mind. She really did want me to go. Take three deep breaths and ask. They can't shout at me while I'm on the phone. They only ever did that behind closed doors.

"It's Claire on the phone," I said nervously. "She's asking me to ask you if

I can go to the disco on Friday?"

"I know who it is, you thick, stupid little bastard," Enid hissed, "It was me who answered the phone. I've already told you, you're not going" she added. As if that wasn't bad enough, HE then got angry.

"Get off that fucking phone, Leon. No wonder you don't get to do anything, when you act bloody clever showing off in front of people.

You're not going and that's it," he said with spiteful hate in his voice. I put the phone down slowly. They had done it again. They had ruined my chance of being normal. I just wanted to be normal.

I just wanted my own mum and dad. Real ones. Why couldn't I have my own mum and dad?

Jim and Enid always rammed down our throats how lucky we were; how grateful we should be that we weren't in one of those children's homes where you have to share a dormitory with 20 or so other boys and girls; where you are made to scrub floors all day and have porridge for every meal. The rest of the time you're locked inside.

A miniature prison.

Why did we listen to them and believe everything they told us about those places? Watching "*Oliver Twist*" on television one weekend must have given them so much satisfaction.

"Told you that's what a kids' home is like," Jim said with a smirk on his face. That was that then. Stay here to be degraded and put down at any given opportunity or, go to one of those children's homes and become a prisoner. What a choice!

I'm here. I've found it. I'm standing outside Anthony's house. All of a sudden it dawns on me that I've not even panicked about being caught -   until now. What if Anthony turns me away, or worse, his Mum calls the police? Well, it's too late now. I'm here. I walk to the back door, because they don't use the front one. I knock at the door. A figure appears behind the smoked glass. It's Anthony.

"What the fuck are you doing here!" he exclaims with a look of complete shock on his face. "I bet I'm the last person you expected to see, eh?" I reply. You see, because Anthony is my best friend at school - my only friend at school – he knows that the only reason for me being at his door right now must be because I have run away.

"You've run away haven't you? Shit Leon, you can't stay here, my mum will hit the roof," he says without hesitation. Just then, a voice calls out from inside his house.

"Anthony, who is it?" his Mum shouts from the living room where she sits and watches television every day and night, only ever moving to empty the ashtray, full of Berkeley Menthol cigarette butts.

"It's o.k. it's just David," Anthony answers quickly.

"Oh! Hiya, David, love," Mary replies.

"Right, we need to move fast. If she realises that it's you, she'll phone the police".

I panic. My heart starts racing. We run for what seems like miles. Anthony says he knows of a place where I can sleep that night. A building is being built next to the main park in Kensom. That building is in clear view now. We slow down until we come to a standstill. We enter the building site.

I'm getting cold now.

"Right, I'll bring you some food and stuff in the morning. O.K. Stay here and whatever you do don't come back out until I tell you it's safe. The police are probably looking for you by now. Fuck, Leon, you really do know how to cause a drama don't you!" Anthony said with a half-smile.

So, here I am, surrounded by bricks, cement and rolls of polythene. There isn't even a roof over this place. What if it rains? I'm starting to feel down. I console myself by talking to my 'other' me.

"You had to do it, Leon. This is a game of survival. He would have destroyed you, if you had stayed another minute," I tell my 'other' me.

Then my mind flashes back to the guy in the car. What was that feeling? I wish he was here now to look after me and keep me safe. He wouldn't mess with my mind and make me feel like a piece of useless filth and scum.

I can't sleep here; the ground is freezing and rock hard. I hate the outdoors.

And I know why.

The previous year, I had gone on a trip to The Lake District with my new school. One of the school teachers who went with us hadn't even wanted me there. She told me as soon as she found out that I was on her excursion that she wouldn't be standing for "any of my crap". I was cheeky at school, you see, trying to show off to the rest of the class. The other kids took great joy in hearing me be "mouthy" to the teachers, and then, they would take a back seat when the punishment was handed out. Therefore, prewarned, I went on the trip on my best behaviour; I just had to prove that I could be a good kid, too.

With eight other pupils, my form teacher, Mr. Flint, and the teacher from hell, we set off up to a slate mine. It was freezing cold, wet and miserable. Once we reached the top, some of the others started messing around. I was determined not to join in, so, by slowly walking backwards and minding my own business, I took in the views.

"Aaarrgh, you bitch," I yelled. Suddenly a sharp, stabbing pain ripped through the side of my head.

"What's happening? I can't see," I screamed. "Help me, please!" I pleaded.

Everything went black.

When I opened my eyes I didn't understand where I was. Why was I in hospital? What was going on?

I'd been hit on the side of the head with a piece of slate that one of the other girls was using to play discus and, because I'd been walking backwards in my own little world, I had walked right into her while in full swing of her throwing the slate. My head had to be stapled to my skull as the cut was too deep. To this day, I still sport a two-inch dent in the left side of my head. The teacher from hell was being so pleasant to me.

Wow! She did have a caring side after all. Next day, my foster parents arrived to take me home early from the vacation. They were fine with me for a few days after that, then, as the bruising started to heal, their nastiness started to break through. All I received from them after that were remarks such as, "You better make sure you get that insurance form I filled in for what happened to your face. We are due compensation for that. You could have lost your eye. How could we look after you then eh? It's always something with you isn't it? Why can't you just stay out of trouble?"

Ironic, isn't it! The one time I stay out of trouble I end up nearly losing an eye, and my foster parents even manage to twist that in such a way that it looks like my fault again. Always my fault!

I'm pathetic!

A waste of space!

I'm not surprised that my natural father committed suicide when I was born. He'd had my sister for two years before I was born and then, as soon as I came along, it became too much and he killed himself.

Why was I even here?

For what possible reason could I be put on this earth?

Was it to suffer?

Was it to pay?

Pay for what, though? More pain was to come my way. Unimaginable pain!

It's getting even colder now. I wonder what time it is, now? I'm not even tired, just cold.

"If I walk around the park for a while I might warm up," I tell myself. The wind is picking up quite a bit and the sound of the polythene blowing begins to scare me. I get up and make my way to the centre of the park. I'm not getting any warmer. I've never been out at this time of night before, yet, even though I'm cold, I feel free. In the centre of the park I notice a long bench that looks very inviting as tiredness begins to take hold. I lie down on it and stare up at the stars.

"I wonder if my real mum is still alive?" I ask my 'other' me.

Just then I hear a noise.

Footsteps.

"Shit!" I whisper, "Someone's coming. What will I do? If I run they will see me. God! Please keep me safe. Don't let anyone hurt me. Not now that I'm free."

I closed my eyes hoping that whoever it was would just go past and not notice me there. A few minutes passed, but it felt like hours. I was squeezing my eyes so tightly shut at this point that I thought they were going to disappear into the back of my head.

I felt someone standing over me.

I knew only too well how that felt.

I wet the bed most nights, right up until the age of eleven or twelve. I can remember, vividly, one occasion when I was only eight years old, lying in my bed and feeling that the sheets were damp.

"Oh no!" I cursed myself. I'd done it again.

I had my favourite pyjamas on that night. The linen ones which felt a bit rough on my skin, but I didn't mind, because they had a large, red racing car on the front. They were great!

I'd done it again; I'd wet the bed. It was the middle of the night and it was pitch black and I was scared to move because I was afraid of the dark. That was the whole reason I persistently kept wetting the bed. I would wake up and just lie there bursting for the toilet, but too scared to move; I would just let it out and lie in it for the rest of the night, in the hope that it would be dry by the morning. Then, a light would come on.

"Shit!" I'd whisper to my 'other' me. It would be one of them coming to feel my sheets. This was normal procedure for me now. They would feel my sheets while I slept. The only reason I knew this was because I got dragged from my bed and thrown onto my bedroom floor one night and hit so many times that I almost passed out with the pain.

But that wasn't the worst occasion.

"I'll just lie here and pretend to be asleep. Maybe they won't notice" I told myself over and over.

I could sense someone leaning over me. It was him; I could tell from the heavy breathing, which had been caused from years of smoking. I felt the hand move under my sheets, moving frantically to find a damp patch so that he would have reason to punish me.

Thud!

My tiny body was again flung onto my bedroom floor. Again, I was made to feel like some kind of dirty animal.

"If you were a cat or a dog I would wipe your face in that, you scummy little twat," my foster dad snarled. "You're a dirty, filthy bastard. You do know that I'm going to have to punish you now, don't you? You leave me no choice" he added.

I knew what was coming next.

"Do you think I enjoy this? Well? Do you? Fucking answer me!" he screamed. I started to cry, he frightened me when he shouted.

Smack! The sting of his big hand slamming down on my piss-drenched skin stung so much. Smack! He hit me again.

Smack!

Smack!

Smack!

Again,

Again,

Again ……..and again. Raining blows to my legs, arms, face, head. Anywhere that he could harm me the most.

"Jim, STOP!" Enid screamed. Even she had a look of terror on her face as he repeatedly punched and slapped me.

"Get the bath run," he screamed at her as he dragged me down the hallway and bumped me down the four steps leading to the bathroom.

"Get in, then!" he demanded. Another cold bath and the nail scrubber to " clean the filth" from my dirty body as he would say.

I fell into a heap on the floor. Cowering and whimpering like a dog. But that's all I was to him. A dog, a stray, that he felt had been put upon him.

What had he done to deserve me?

So here I was, closing my eyes tight, someone leaning over me. Was this person going to hurt me? Suddenly, a man's voice broke through my thoughts.

"What you doing here?" demanded the rough voice.

Quickly, I opened my eyes, and, realising that there was no escape, I blurted out the truth.

"I've run away from home and I was going to stay at my friend's house but I can't in case his Mum phones the police and I get taken back home"

I blurted it out in such a rush that I was surprised he understood anything I was saying.

"What did you run away for?" he questioned.

"I live with my mum and dad who aren't my real mum and dad. They don't really want me there, and, I hate them both so much," I answered.

"Where you going to run to?" he asked.

I shrugged my shoulders to indicate that I didn't know what I was going to do.

"You can come and stay with me and my girlfriend if you want" he said.

"Can I?" I answered with such surprise in my voice.

"Who's your mate anyway?" he asked. "Anthony Sharpe" I answered,

"Do you know him?"

"Who? Sharpey! God aye, I know Sharpey," he answered. "How old are you?" he added. I looked at him and then again, from nowhere, came that same feeling that I'd had with the other man in the car. What was this? Was it because I felt good that these men were nice to me? The only other man in my life was a complete monster and yet I craved his attention.

"I'm fourteen" I replied.

"Well, don't worry, mate; I'll look after you. Come on, it's not far to mine" he encouraged, in a caring, but masculine voice.

His name was Jamie. He was so manly: quite rough- looking, but attractive. I felt safe with this stranger. When you have been abused physically and mentally by the two people who are meant to love and protect you, a kind stranger becomes your best friend. As he did…….. for now.

We didn't say much while we were walking to his place, yet it didn't feel as though these were uncomfortable silences.

I remember thinking, "Is this what a boy should feel like with his Dad?" A big, strong dad who looks after his pride and joy; keeping him safe, taking him fishing. Even though I didn't like fishing I would have pretended I did, just to spend all my time with MY DAD.

But I couldn't. My dad was dead. He left me on this earth to struggle along, battling with my emotions, feeling lonely without escape from my tortured mind and broken spirit, unable to trust anyone other than my 'other' me.

But then, as always after feeling anger towards him, I become sad. He wasn't to know I would suffer at the hands of a monster and that it would leave me emotionally scarred and confused towards men, constantly craving their attention.

We arrived at Jamie's house and when we walked inside, Jamie introduced me to his girlfriend. I don't remember her name, so I shall call her Debbie. I only recall two of the seven evenings spent here, for some reason. The first evening I remember feeling very relaxed and a thousand miles away from the nightmare I'd left behind. I was really tired and Debbie suggested that I sleep on the sofa, as their two-year old daughter's room only had a cot in it. I was more than happy. I couldn't believe how friendly they were both being towards me. After I had told her a little of my past, Debbie told me that I could stay with them as long as I wanted.

Wow!

This was my first night of freedom.

I couldn't remember the last time I had been able to fall asleep without my stomach churning, wondering if I'd be woken up through the night to be accused of something and be punished accordingly. What an amazing feeling not having to answer to anyone! Not having to ask for permission to use the toilet!

We'd always had to ask to use the toilet for as long as I could remember.

"Can I go to the toilet, please?" I would ask sheepishly.

"Hurry up, then, and straight back down these stairs when you're finished!" they would reply. They were so predictable.

If I was longer than the usual time of about two and a half minutes I would be bombarded with "What have you been up to up there?" or "I told you to come straight down when you'd finished" followed by "When will you do as you're bloody told!"

But there was one time after asking and getting the usual answer, I rushed to the toilet, had a quick pee, then, ran down the stairs as fast as I could. I couldn't have taken longer than a minute this time. When I re-appeared through the living room door Jim looked at me with a slight smirk on his face and then demanded, "What were you doing?"

"I was at the toilet," I answered.

"Don't get fucking lippy," he snarled, and then he left the room for what could only have been a few minutes.

Suddenly the living room door swung open and he stood in the doorway, eyes bulging, wild with fury.

"RIGHT! You little twat" he screamed, holding out his hand.

"What?" I whispered, cowering into the sofa. My mind raced. What had I done now? I only went to the toilet. I promised myself that's all I'd done.

"You haven't done anything," I frantically told my 'other' me. "You haven't, you haven't," I repeated over and over.

Then............Darkness would fall.

My mind would always cut out when I knew he was playing one of his sick and twisted games. It was my way of saving my 'other' me, because if he got to that part of me then I would be finished, beaten.

"Who snapped these off the plant?" he demanded, showing my sister and me some flower buds in his large, cracked hand. We both shrugged our shoulders.

"Well, someone done it" he sneered.

"Was it you?" he asked looking at Beverly.

"No," she answered, her voice shaking.

"Well it must have been you, then," he said accusingly.

"It wasn't," I answered. But what was the point in even saying it wasn't me when, in his sick head, he had already planned this with only one ending in mind. Out came the brown, leather belt with the thick buckle attached to it. We knew the procedure, but he took pleasure in telling us it again anyway.

"Right then, come on. Kitchen. NOW!" he demanded, "Who's first?"

By saying" who's first", he meant who wants to bend over the kitchen chair and have their spindly legs smashed against a large buckle. I felt sick.

My sister was pleading, backing away from the chair.

"Please don't, Dad," she pleaded.

He raised his arm quickly to test her reflexes, to see if she was frightened enough to flinch.

She was.

"Just get over the fucking chair. Now! Do it. Over the chair"

"PLEASE" my sister screamed.

"Over the chair; OVER THE FUCKING CHAIR!" he screamed, pure rage taking over his face.

"It was me! It was me" I screamed.

He folded his belt away slowly.

"See the trouble your brother causes," he said, looking at my frightened sister, then, turning to me, he added, "Get to bed".

I dragged myself up the stairs, my own frail body becoming too much to hold up anymore. I felt so tired. Not yet a teenager and, yet, wishing I was dead, so that the pain would stop. Disgusted with myself, yet again, for admitting to something for which I knew neither my sister nor I were guilty.

I wonder when it first started?

I can remember as far back to the ages of around seven or eight. I do have two memories of happier times. The first memory is when Mum and I would go over the road to the grocery shop and she would buy me a Mr. Men cake. It was a little round sponge cake with an edible picture on top, glued together with icing.

Where did that kind mum go?

At what point did things change?

My second memory was when I was about six -maybe seven- and we were at Lantern Wildlife Park. I was sitting in the sun eating an ice-lolly and felt something behind me. It was a reindeer and, without warning, it swiped the ice-lolly from my hand and galloped off with it. I was in tears, so my foster dad bought me another. Again, I ask myself and try so hard to remember,

At what point did things change?

Why do we need to ask to use the toilet for God's sake!

…"Radio one FM. Your choice of music coming right up," the radio

blares.

"Wakey, wakey sleepy head" Debbie says, holding a cup of tea.

"Thank you," I reply, taking it from her small hand. I feel like I'm dreaming.

I've been away from that hell-hole for a whole night! Oh my God, I can't believe I've done it. I've escaped; and I'm never going back.

Never!

"What do you fancy doing today then?" asked Jamie swaggering through the living room door and playfully ruffling my hair on the way past.

"I've got my very own bodyguard", I thought to myself excitedly, "a man who's going to look after me and protect me. Mine." No one could spoil this moment. I really felt as though I'd walked into a dream.

"Dunno," I answered. I didn't care what we did. We could sit there in that room all day. I'd be happy to do whatever, as long as it was next to my bodyguard.

"You can help me pick some mushrooms tonight" said Jamie.

"O.K." I answered innocently.

Debbie threw a stern glance to Jamie.

"What?" he said looking at her with a cheeky grin on his face.

"You know what, Jamie. You know I don't want you doing that" she snapped.

"Chill out, man, it'll be fine," he said, shrugging his shoulders. That whole conversation went right over my head! The day flew by in a haze of happiness. Loud dance music on the cassette player in the kitchen and cigarettes being smoked whenever I fancied having one. This was truly amazing.

The time was about 10pm. It was growing dark now and Jamie was starting to fidget on the sofa.

"Come on then, kid," he said to me, springing on to his feet.

"Just watch yourself, eh, and don't be long," Debbie shouted to us as we fled out of the back door through the kitchen.

We were going to pick mushrooms. Quite late to pick mushrooms, I thought to myself.

"You ever had magic mushrooms, kid?" asked Jamie.

"No. I've had fried ones," I answered.

Jamie fell to the floor in fits of laughter.

"What?" I asked, innocently.

"Nowt! You just make me laugh," he said, still laughing.

"Now, these are the mushrooms we need to pick," he said pointing to the funny, small, pointed mushrooms scattered in clumps across the large Bowling Club lawn. We spent the next hour picking them and then started to head back to his place. He began to roll some of the mushrooms into little balls.

"What you doing that for?" I asked inquisitively.

"Well, you roll them into little balls and swallow them. Then, after half an hour or so you start to hallucinate" he replied.

I didn't have a clue what he was talking about. That was one of the good points of being kept in the house and not being let out of sight. I was still innocent with regard to drugs! I asked him what the word 'hallucinate' meant.

"It just means you take something to be able to see things that aren't there. Like cartoons and stuff" he said.

I didn't see the point in that, so, when he offered me some, I turned him down.

By the time we arrived back at the house, he was wasted. He just looked drunk and I didn't feel threatened. Debbie sent him off to bed and then she sat down next to me on the sofa. She'd been drinking.

"You know he's bisexual don't you?" she slurred.

"Yeah, course I do" I answered, trying not to look the least bit surprised.

"Oh, my God! IS HE?" I thought excitedly.

Why was I getting excited?

Was I gay?

No way. I hated gays. They were people who died from that gay disease weren't they? I started to get a hard on. I knew what bisexual meant. I'd read it in a book called 'The Joy of Sex' that was sitting on the bookshelf at home. I had taken so much interest in it that I'd done further research on it to find a clearer meaning and looked it up in the dictionary.

"Doesn't it bother you?" she asked, still slurring her words.

I shrugged my shoulders as if to say, " Dunno".

"Anyway, I'm off to bed, sweetheart. See you in the morning" she said, getting up.

"Night" I replied.

My mind was racing.

Excited.

Confused.

Shocked.

I thought all gay people acted like girls. He was 100% pure man: a bricklayer; a rough lad from the council estate in Kensom. He'd been in prison and everything. How could he be gay? She'd been drunk and can't have meant it. Anyway, how could I bring that up in conversation?

"Er, by the way, your girlfriend told me you're a poof".

I don't think so.

I tried to forget about it, as I lay down on the sofa ready to face another day of freedom at Jamie and Debbie's house.

I fell asleep in no time at all.

Sunshine was sneaking through the crack in between the living room curtains, strips of heated brightness beating down on my face. Another day of freedom! I never stopped being surprised by this feeling. Long may it last.

"Where is everyone?" I muttered to my 'other' self. There was no noise at all until 'thud'. I jumped.

"What the hell was that?" I said out loud. I didn't think I'd said it that loudly, but I must have, because, from somewhere upstairs, Jamie replied, "It's all right, it's just the postman. Fetch it up, bud" he went on.

I got up and went to the front door where there was a parcel lying on the mat. I picked it up and made my way up the stairs. Jamie was lying in the bed with the covers just below his waist. I couldn't stop looking.

"What you looking at? Are you queer?" he said.

"What?" I replied in an awkward tone.

"I'm joking with you, mate! Pass me the post," he said laughing.

I must have gone a bright shade of purple because I was so embarrassed!

I passed him the post then turned to go back down the stairs.

"Do you fancy going to London tomorrow?" he asked, quite matter of fact.

"London?" I answered, "I don't have any money to go to London" I added.

"Don't worry about money, I'm going anyway, so I want you to come with me; the police will never find you there. I've got a mate there where we can stay, so it'll be all right, bud. You fancy it? Just you and me?" he said smiling.

"YES!" I said excitedly.

I couldn't believe it. We were going to London! I'd been there when I was nine or ten to see the Queen doing a public appearance on the streets outside Buckingham Palace. London is the place where the Queen lives in a massive palace; there's a toyshop called Hamleys and it's the size of a whole street! It has every single type of toy, sweet and game available in the world. Miniature cars that kids can really drive!

Here I was in Jamie's bedroom being asked by MY very own bodyguard if I wanted to go with him to London! I wanted to jump up and down with excitement, jump on his bed, give him a huge hug, feel his strong arms wrap around my skinny body, making me feel safe, making me feel loved, making me feel wanted.

Was I dreaming? Was this really happening to me?

Yes it was.

But, with every dream comes the nightmares.

With every pleasure comes a pain more frightening than the mind can ever begin to imagine.

I was soon to discover that, up until this point, my life had been a walk in the park.

The rest of the day flew by in a blur of smiles and excitement. When I lay down on the sofa to fall asleep I couldn't. It was hopeless, I was too excited and I would have to resort to the 'Christmas trick'. The Christmas trick was a great way to ensure you would get to sleep quickly on Christmas Eve even though you weren't tired. Every Christmas Eve, Beverly and I would get a blob of toothpaste from the tube and rub some of it under each eye. Within minutes, our eyes would sting if we tried to keep them open. Tears would stream down our faces as we made our way to our beds, half-blinded. This made sure we kept them tightly closed and, before we knew it, it would be morning time. I'm not sure where the idea came from - or if it was even safe – but, nights like tonight, I didn't care as long as it worked.

I went to the bathroom and smudged two thick lines of toothpaste under each eye. "Yes!" I screamed out as the tears started rolling down my face.

I stumbled back to the sofa.

It was morning.

I was woken up by screams of "We're going to London. Who's going to London? Leon and Jamie! We're going to London today!" sung in a football style song that all of the supporters scream and shout during one of the games.

"Come on then, kid. We'll have some breakfast and then we'd better get going. The train is in an hour. Here's a pair of jeans and some tops, try 'em on and see if they fit you. Hopefully they will and we can bring 'em with us for you to wear." Jamie said throwing a pile of clothes at me.

"Cool" I replied. I hope they do fit, I thought to myself trying them on; anything to get a bit closer to Jamie.

They did fit. I was really happy.

We sat and ate some cereal and then Debbie started to make us some toast while Jamie went upstairs to get his bags.

"You remember what I said the other night. O.K. Just be careful, and promise me you will remind Jamie to send me the money for the train tickets. He's used his own daughter's savings for this bloody holiday!" she added in a bitter tone.

"Sorry" I mumbled, "I didn't know it was hers."

"That's not your fault. I'm just letting you know, that's all" she replied, giving me a hug "Look after yourself and I'll see you soon".

What she said the other night? It must be true then. I thought she had just had too much to drink. So he was bisexual. He hadn't tried anything yesterday when she was out because I was too young I told myself. I felt strange though. Almost as though I was upset that he hadn't.

Jamie came to the front door, interrupting our hug.

"What you two talking about?" he asked in a suspicious way.

"Nothing," snapped Debbie, "I was just telling Leon to enjoy his holiday"

"Come on, mate, we need to be going", he said to me, while still giving Debbie a dirty look.

Debbie smiled at Jamie in a cocky way, tilting her head sideways. She obviously wasn't happy about us going, but I just didn't pick up on it at that stage.

It's only looking back now that I see why she wasn't happy.

She was trying to protect me.

We said our goodbyes and headed for the train station.

My heart was thumping with fear as we drew closer to the station. Apart from the night I'd helped Jamie pick mushrooms, I'd not been out of the house. What if the police were waiting at the station?

We'd checked the local news and newspapers every day to see if I had been mentioned but there had been nothing.

We arrived at the station and there was our train sitting at the platform.

"Run!" Jamie shouted, half dragging me on to the train.

The whistle blew. We were off. We were on our way to London!

During the first hour of the journey I had dozed on and off. I was wide awake now, though.

"What was she saying to you in the kitchen?" asked Jamie.

"Nowt much," I replied. Do I tell him what she said? What if he thinks that I'm lying to him and gets mad and hits me?

"Just tell me," he said.

"Well," I said hesitantly, pausing.

"Well what? Come on, just tell me," he demanded looking straight at me.

"She said you were.... Well.... you know.... Like....she said that you go with ....men," I spluttered out nervously.

"Does that bother you like?" he asked.

"Er, no" I answered.

"Cool," he said. He fell asleep.

My heart jumped about ten beats! It was true. I couldn't believe it. I don't think that I had actually believed that it might be true. Why was I so bothered anyway? I'd never looked at men and 'fancied' them.

Or had I?

Is that what I felt for that guy when I got into his car for a lift? I'd thought he was good looking. Did that mean I'd 'fancied' him?

I was really confused about what I felt for Jamie now and sat daydreaming about it in my own little world until a clinking noise snapped me out of it.

"Refreshments" said the tall man peering over me. I woke Jamie to ask him if he wanted anything.

"Do you like Cherryade?" Jamie asked me.

"I love it," I answered.

"Cool," he said, smiling at me.

"A bottle of your Cherryade, mate," he said turning to the tall man.

"Haven't got any Cherryade, only got Lemonade, Cola or Orange Crush" he said, looking back at Jamie.

"Should we get Cola? I can't stand the other two," he said to me.

"Yeah" I answered.

We sat and shared the bottle of Cola. It tasted just like the pop we got at home from the pop man.

The pop man would come round the houses with crates of pop every second Monday, taking back the crate full of the empty bottles from the week before and replacing it with full ones. We ordered a mixture of flavours. Well, I say WE, what I meant was that Jim had a mixture of flavours. The crate would comprise of twelve bottles: two each of

Cherryade, Orange Crush, Limeade, Lime Crush, Cream Soda and then one of Cola and one of Raspberryade. The Orange Crush, Cream Soda and Limeade belonged to Jim; the Cherryade and Raspberryade belonged to Enid. I remember once asking to taste the Cream Soda. The reply I received was no surprise.

"Fuck off! You can't see nowt going past your face without wanting it, can you!" Jim snarled, "You've got two different flavours to choose from" he added, still snarling.

We were allowed the Lime Crush and the Cola. The Lime Crush tasted like shit! That was the only reason we were allowed it, because they didn't like it. Weren't we lucky!

Of course we were. After all "Not all kids get pop delivered to the door.

You don't know how lucky you two little bastards are. Do you think you would get pop in an orphanage?

Eh? I can tell you right now, there's no chance you would, so stop being so fucking greedy!" he would say.

It was towards the end of the second week and the pop man would be back on Monday but we still had a full bottle of that skanky Lime Crush left in the crate. I decided that, if I sneaked it out with me to school I could show off with it and, God forbid, maybe make some friends. I'd realized, by this point, even at primary school, that fake friends were better than no friends.

How would I sneak it out though?

We were searched every morning before leaving the house for school.

Enid would rub her hands up and down our uniforms, front and back, and then Jim would search our school bags. He would always find something to throw out of it saying "You're not taking that to school. You're there to learn, not piss about"

To this day, I can't see why having a sticker in my schoolbag from the dentist was 'Pissing about' as he would put it.

How would I get the bottle out?

"I've got it!" I whispered to myself excitedly.

My heart was racing so fast I caught myself gasping for breath. "It's only a bottle of pop" I told myself. I opened the back door as quietly as I could - with difficulty, though, as the door needed oiled.

"If I get caught I'm dead meat" I thought as I slid out of the back door. I needed to make it to the next door, which was in the back yard that led to the lane running behind the row of ten houses to which we were central…

Sweat is dripping from my forehead like a tap, which makes it difficult to see and takes my mind off the job in hand. I'm so frightened that I might get caught; a nervous sickly feeling takes over my body, running through my veins like poison. Just as I make it to the door in the yard, my hand barely pushing down the green painted metal latch, I hear something.

"Shit" I whisper so sharply, it cuts through the silent air like a thunder storm piercing the skies.

"Someone's coming, someone's coming, someone's coming," I repeat over and over. Footsteps! I hear footsteps. Oh God no, please don't let me get caught!

Just then, I hurl the bottle of pop over the next-door neighbour's wall.

'Thud' it falls on the soft grass. Then………..

"What the hell are you up to?" Enid snarls as she sneaks up behind me.

"Wh…at? I'm….I'm….j…ust checking that…," I say, so nervously I begin to stutter.

"Checking what?" she says so matter- of- fact as if to say, 'I've caught you out, ha, ha, ha, ha!'

"The rubbish; I was just checking the rubbish was out," I say.

"Well, it is! Now get ready for school. NOW!" she yelps.

I race into the house, my heart thumping so fast I'm sure they can see it jumping through my school jumper.

"That was close," I whisper to myself. I wouldn't care; I don't even like the stuff that much!

After being searched, Beverly and I set off, walking to school. As soon as we were out of sight of the window, from which their eyes burned through the back of our heads watching us as we walked, I doubled back and ran as fast as I could to retrieve the bottle of pop.

I was so relieved that it hadn't smashed. I wouldn't be trying that trick again; it was too dangerous.

Finally, we arrived at school and I gained a few new 'friends' for the day and that was that. I went home thinking nothing more of it. It was Wednesday and we finished school on Friday afternoon, so, I thought to myself, I'll sneak the bottle back home then. I couldn't do it that day as Enid was home early from work on a Wednesday and Thursday and the rest of the week passed by.

It was now the weekend. Like most weekends, we went to Pendal to buy the weekly shopping, and then back home to sit and do nothing. I hated the weekends so much, only because Jim didn't work on those two days which meant he was home ALL day AND night. That would be nothing compared to what lay ahead of us. We were on our six-week summer holiday from school!

That weekend passed quite quickly and it was soon Monday. In the early afternoon, the doorbell rang and, when I answered it, there was the pop man.

"Who is it?" Jim shouted out from the kitchen.

"Pop man," I replied.

Suddenly, Jim appeared behind me within seconds of asking who it was, as if he'd already known and was ready to pounce; but why?

"I've not got the old crate ready yet. Can you come back in about an hour for it" asked Jim.

I remember thinking to myself "What's he up to?"

"No bother, mate" replied the pop man "I'll catch you later this afternoon on my second round if that's all right?"

"Perfect" Jim answered with a smirk on his face.

He closed the front door.

It suddenly went dark.

"Aaaarrrgh!" I screamed, pain stabbing at my head.

"WHERE IS IT?" Jim screamed in my face, his eyes going bloodshot as his temper rose.

I couldn't think fast enough. I was becoming more and more disorientated as he struck me again and again over the head with the slipper he'd taken off his foot: anything to cause me more pain.

"WHERE'S THE FUCKING BOTTLE?" he was screaming as he smashed the shoe at my head.

"Please!" I screamed. "It's at school".

"What! I can't hear you" he sneered.

'CLACK' the slipper went as it burned my scalp.

I didn't have time to answer.

'CLACK' it went again.

"I can't hear you," he taunted.

'CLACK! CLACK! CLACK!' three more blows.

With all my might and energy I screamed at the top of my voice

"IT'S AT SCHOOL!"

"And what is it doing in the school? Eh? Answer me that one," he said in a calm and callous voice as if the last five minutes hadn't taken place.

"I took it there" I whispered quietly, slumping to the ground.

He grabbed me by the throat as he knelt down towards me, twisting my face around as he did so, raising it to the level of his own.

"You've got an hour," he said calmly.

I looked at him, confused. What did he mean? I had an hour left? Was he going to kill me? Send me away? What? I really didn't know what was in store for me. Nor did I care anymore. My head was still ringing with the pain from the thumps to the head I'd just received.

"Get that bottle back in this house or you won't know what's hit you," he said half smirking.

This was another one of his sick twisted games. How could I get the bottle back from the school? It was the summer holidays. He knew that.

"But..." I said.

"But?" he said in a questioning voice "But nothing. You've got an hour".

What was I going to do? I got up from the floor, brushing down the crumbs that had stuck to my bare legs as I had been battered with the slipper.

What did I do to make him hate me so much?

I only wanted him to love me. That was all.

I went out of the front door, not knowing what to do to make this entire nightmare disappear.

I walked down the street, heading towards the school. The walk to school usually took fifteen minutes. I remember thinking about running away then but the fear of what he would do to me when I was caught was so much more terrifying that I decided it wasn't an option.

"The school is closed," I hissed to my 'other' me, as tears ran down my face. I cursed myself for still being alive and for being so stupid.

Why did I keep screwing things up? I had no-one to blame but myself this time. I took the bottle to school to make fake 'friends' and in the process I had caused myself to be given a thorough battering. Yet, that was nothing compared to what would happen to me if I returned home without the bottle.

I reached the school grounds and had a look around for the caretaker.

There was nobody there. The school was completely deserted. I walked around the empty playground, scratching at my legs as they burned in the heat from the sun.

"What do I do?" I asked my 'other' me.

"Try and get into the classroom," I answered.

It was the only way. I had to get that bottle back. I just had to.

A loud, crashing sound echoed through the playground as I hurled a brick through my classroom window.

Quickly, I crawled through the tiny window. It was barely big enough and I almost became trapped, wriggling through it. Within seconds I was in my classroom, frantically racing over to where I'd so stupidly left the bottle on the Friday.

"Got it!" I said, my voice rushing with adrenalin.

I tucked the bottle half way between my shorts and my tee-shirt, climbed up the ledge towards the window and started to wriggle back through it.

A sudden, sharp pain seared through my left leg. I looked back, half hanging out of the window to see my leg pinned to the window by a large shard of glass.

Then, suddenly, from nowhere, came a gruff voice.

"HEY!" the voice echoed from a distance. Obviously close enough to see someone half hanging from the school window.

"Oh, my God! I've been caught," I shrieked to myself.

Panicking, I pulled and pulled at my leg, screaming in pain as my flesh tore open to reveal a three-inch hole. Blood was spraying in every direction.

I dropped to the ground crashing my knees and hands on the concrete as I landed. Without even thinking, I leapt onto my feet and ran. I kept running until I was half- way home. I still don't know to this day who it was who shouted out as I hung from the school window. Blood was pouring down my leg as I limped home. How was I going to explain this? Simple, I thought to myself. I'll say that I tripped up as I was running home and fell on some glass.

I walked in the front door.

He was standing in the hallway waiting for me to get back.

"How did you get that?" he growled, snatching the bottle from my hand as I cowered past him.

"The school was open," I replied sheepishly.

"LIAR" he shouted.

He knew exactly what I'd done. He knew I would have needed to break into the classroom. It was the summer holidays.

"Tell me the truth," he demanded.

I told him that the school had been closed because it was the summer holidays and that I'd had to smash the window to get into the classroom to get the bottle back.

"Little BASTARD!" he shouted, smacking me so hard across the back that I fell over.

I screamed in pain, begging for him to leave me alone.

He didn't listen.

"Get your shorts down!" he demanded, pulling the kitchen chair into the middle of the floor.

"No please" I begged over and over "I'm sorry"

"Sorry for what" he snapped.

"I'm sorry. I'm sorry for taking the bottle," I said, sobbing   uncontrollably.

"Shut that fucking crying up" he demanded as he flung me over the chair.

"Please.........PLEASE" I screamed.

My body was ready to give in.

The pain was too much.

My head ringing from the belting of the slipper only an hour earlier, the throbbing from the gaping wound in my leg, my back stinging from the slap I'd just got for lying.

Pain tore through every part of my skinny body.

I went limp; hanging over the chair like a rag doll.

Time for more punishment.

Time for the leather belt.

Blackout.

The belt thrashed my legs. I screamed with every blow as the buckle ripped through my skin. This was the worst pain I'd ever felt. After what seemed like a lifetime he stopped and told me to pull my shorts up. I thought at that moment I was going to be sick. Before I knew it, I felt it rise up my throat like a snake. I kept my mouth tightly closed as it spread over my tongue and gushed through my teeth. I swallowed it back down for the fear of being hit again for being sick on the floor.

He stood staring at me in utter disgust.

"That's what you get for theft," he said with no remorse for what he'd just done.

I looked at the floor. Then he spoke again.

"What did we do to deserve you?" he said in a voice that made him sound like a victim.

I shrugged my shoulders.

Yet again he had won his sick little game. Demanding I bring home the bottle I'd 'stolen' from the crate, threatening me that if I came back without it I would be 'for it!' Then, knowing I would come back with it because I didn't want to get leathered, he would leather me anyway, for breaking into the school.

I still haven't drunk another sip of that skanky Lime Crush to this very day!

"Are you o.k. kid?" a familiar voice asks.

My thoughts are back to the present.

Here I am, on my way to the big city lights.

I still couldn't believe how lucky I was to be getting far away from my past life. I hoped Beverly was o.k. I wondered if she'd run away? Probably not: she was always less rebellious than me.

The train slows down and then comes to a complete standstill.

"Come on then, kid. Get your bag, we need to get off," says Jamie, in a protective voice.

"We've made it!" I whisper with tears in both eyes.

Jamie gives me a huge hug.

We get off the train and are faced with what looks like a stampede of people coming towards us.

"What's happening?" I ask with panic in my voice.

"Nothing, kid, this is how London is all the time. Everyone in a rush to get nowhere," Jamie replied.

I didn't like this at all. Sudden panic gripped my mind. What was I doing so far away from home? Had I made a mistake? Yet, surely this was better than being battered black and blue for the slightest thing. Why was I beginning to feel so uncomfortable?

"Where's your friend?" I asked Jamie.

"He'll be here soon. Stop panicking" he replied in a soft voice.

I wished I could, indeed, stop panicking. I think the enormity of what I had done began to hit me right there in the middle of London Euston station.

About fifteen minutes passed by. My eyes were darting all over the station, watching people, wondering who they were, where they were going. Had they all run away from home too?

"Here's Michael now" said Jamie. A tall skinny man with a kind face walked towards us.

"I told you there was nothing to panic about," Jamie said, as he ruffled the hair on the back of my head.

Jamie introduced me to Michael and then we all headed out of the station towards a car park where Michael had parked his car.

We were in the car for about forty minutes and, during the journey, Jamie explained to Michael that I'd ran away from home because my foster parents had been beating me. He didn't go in to much more detail than that. Michael then told me that he, too, had a foster son called Anthony who was seventeen and he finished the conversation by turning to me and saying that I could stay there for as long as I wanted, but only on the condition that I phoned home in a few days time to let them know that I was o.k.

Hesitantly, I agreed.

Michael's house was on three floors. When we walked in the front door we were facing the kitchen, then, on the first floor was the living room and a bedroom, on the second floor was another bedroom and the bathroom. The first floor bedroom was

Anthony's; he shared it with his 'friend,' David. The second bedroom was Michael's; he shared that with his 'partner', Jamie.

"You two can share this room," Michael said as he showed us into the living room.

"You can pull out the sofa, it turns into a double bed," he added.

A double bed! Oh my God, I'm going to be sharing a bed with Jamie.

I couldn't believe it. I wanted to be close to Jamie so much. I didn't know why, or what I was feeling at this point, and I didn't care.

It was about eleven o' clock by now and Jamie suggested we go to bed.

My heart was racing as we pulled the bed out and put the bedding on the sofa. Anthony popped his head round the living room door and started smiling.

"What's funny?" asked Jamie.

"Don't get up to anything I wouldn't do!" he said laughing.

"Piss off" Jamie snapped as he threw a cushion at the door.

I lay down in the makeshift bed and Jamie turned the light out and crawled in beside me. There was a space between us and I desperately wanted to feel his skin next to mine. I wanted him to hold me and keep me warm.

In the midst of these thoughts, Jamie started to whisper to me.

"Have you ever touched a lad's cock?" he asked, in a hushed voice.

I froze immediately. My whole body became tense and my head began to thump. What do I say to that?

What if it's a trick and then, if I go to touch him, he thumps me? I didn't think it would be a trick, but I doubted myself so much; all the time in fact.

When someone has screwed with your head as much as Jim and Enid had done with mine, you begin to doubt everything. At times it's like you are going crazy. When someone constantly tells you that you have said something or taken something you begin to wonder if, indeed, you have done what they say.

After all, why would your dad take his own money out of his wallet and then try to blame one of you for it going missing? He was constantly toying with your emotions, keeping you on a constant guard. That's when I had found my friend who helped me through the really bad times: the person I refer to as my 'other' me. My 'other' me was the one who kept me sane, the one who taught me to question people's motives. The one who made me realise that I wasn't going mad and that just because adults persist in telling you that you are 'stupid', 'thick', 'ugly', 'scum', a 'liar', a 'thief', an 'orphan', and any other derogatory words they could possibly find to try and suppress or even break your spirit, that it doesn't make it true.

However, now I've put myself in a truly dangerous situation: a situation more frightening than anything that had happened previously at home. I am fourteen years old.

I find myself lying next to a thirty year old man and he is asking me if I've touched another lad's cock. I hear my 'other' self, screaming inside my head, "Is this a trick?" and "Be careful" and "What if he hurts you"?

Before I even have time to answer my own questions I feel the bed covers move. My heart is racing, my stomach queasy with sickness. What do I want to happen? I don't know what I want to happen! I want to be looked after and kept safe by MY Jamie.

"I want to be loved," I splutter out loudly.

Did I just say that to my 'other' me?

Just as I thought: No.

Jamie's hand takes hold of my penis.

What's he doing that for? I'm really scared now. What does he want me to do?

"I'll love you," he says in a voice I haven't heard him use before. I felt that because I was the one who had blurted out that I wanted to be loved, there was no going back. I was frightened.

"Take your clothes off," he demanded.

I found myself doing everything he told me to do. Demand after demand followed.

"Put this in your mouth," he said, pushing his penis inside my mouth. The tears rolled down my face as I cried silently in the dark and did as he said.

"Lie down," he said pulling me towards him. He got on top of me and forced me inside him. He groaned louder and faster as he bounced roughly up and down on my penis.

It hurt so much. A thousand things were running through my mind.

When will he stop?

I'm really sore.

Why is it hard if I don't like it?

Does this mean he loves me?

That must mean my dad DIDN'T love me. He didn't want to do this to me. He'd only wanted Beverly in his room when Enid was at work. Is this what they had being doing in the bedroom? I lay there becoming increasingly limp as the pain in my penis became worse. I had to think of a way to make it stop.

"I need the toilet," I said, holding back the shaking in my voice so that he wouldn't suspect that anything was wrong.

Quickly, I ran up the stairs to the toilet. I just sat there, staring at the bathroom floor wondering what to do next.

"Go for a drink" I whispered to my 'other' me.

As quickly and as quietly as I could, I sneaked past the living room door and down the stairs to the kitchen. I poured myself some juice from the fridge and sat there, waiting and hoping that this was all a bad dream and that I would wake up in my own bed at home.

Suddenly, the kitchen door flew open and I jumped with sheer terror as Jamie appeared, his muscled body towering over me.

"I'm not finished. You don't just get up and leave," he said in a cold tone.

"My dick hurts a bit," I said, trying hard to look like I'd just being enjoying myself. I knew that if I was good for him then he would love me and look after me, like Jim had started to do with Beverly.

It all started to make sense. All kids must do this. The reason Jim didn't do it with me was because he hated me and liked Beverly more. That's why she got more attention. That's why he wanted to send me away. I had to give Jamie what he wanted, otherwise he wouldn't want me either and then I would have no-one to look after me, protect me and keep me safe.

I followed him back up the stairs and into the living room where the sofa bed lay waiting for me to return to 'finish off'. Jamie wedged himself between my legs and started kissing my face. His stubble burnt my skin as his kissing became more and more intense.

I felt his penis against my buttocks.

Blackout.

When he drove it inside me it stung like putting vinegar on to your chips when you have a cut on your hand. Only this was worse; much worse.

As it penetrated me I felt the inside of my stomach churning. My mind was racing. A feeling of pain; a feeling of belonging. Affectionate pain.

Although it hurt, for that split second it felt like it was worth it because I felt loved and wanted. Wanted. That's all.

He finished between my thighs.

"You're a good ride," he said, then rolled off and went to sleep.

I lay there staring up at the ceiling.

Had I just been raped?

I felt so confused. I can't have been raped. Can I?

I let him do it to me. I could have stopped him couldn't I? Of course I could have done. But deep down I didn't want to stop him. He wanted me. He called me a 'good ride'. At last, I belonged somewhere. I belonged to Jamie.

Every morning became a routine in which Jamie would have sex with me. I would lie there on my back as he pushed himself in and out of me: sometimes it would really hurt the inside of my tummy and other times I became so limp that I didn't feel much at all.

The next two weeks passed by in a blur. I didn't do much through the day, but I do remember always feeling hungry because Michael would be out at work every day and there never seemed to be any food in the fridge. If Jamie was in the house he would always manage to go out and come back with something to eat; but then even this became less regular as he would disappear for hours on end saying he was going to look for some work and that I should stay in the house. Sometimes I would go with him as he looked for building work on the local sites.

Eventually, one day, after being out for a few hours, Jamie came back in to tell me he had a job. I was really happy, because he was happy.

However, another change was to come.

The evening of the day he found a job, Jamie started to gather up his belongings and move them into Anthony's room.

"What are you doing?" I asked.

"Well, I need to get up early now I've got a job and I don't want to wake you up on a morning, so I'm going to stay in Anthony's room because he gets up early as well," he explained.

I was devastated! I didn't even mind him raping me every night, if it meant he would stay in my room. I needed him. Suddenly, all of these thoughts flooded my head:

Is he having sex with Anthony? He is, isn't he! I convinced myself that he was; and I was distraught.

Of course, I was right. However, what I didn't know was that Jamie had already had a discussion with Michael about the sleeping arrangements.

That night I cried myself to sleep. I felt so alone without Jamie next to me, because even though it hurt when he had sex with me, he would always cuddle me afterwards.

"Who's that?" I screamed into the darkness of the room as I bolted upright.

That wasn't Jamie's hand.

I was scared.

"WHO IS IT?" I screamed.

"Sshhhh!" said a voice as a hand came over my mouth to stifle my scream.

I couldn't move. I couldn't speak.

"Aaaaargh!" screamed my 'other' me. These screams, however, were only heard in my head. It was no use. I was trapped.

"Listen! This is my house so do as I say if you want to stop here."

It was a familiar voice.

It was Michael!

Terror gripped my mind. Jamie had moved on to Anthony and told Michael that he could have me, now that he was finished with me. He rammed himself inside me with such force that I bled for the rest of the night.

After what seemed like a lifetime, he finished and pulled out of me, then got up to go back out of the room. He turned to me and I heard him say, in a calm voice, "Jamie said you were a good ride", as he left the room.

Blackout.

I cried myself to sleep clutching my stomach.

The next day I told Jamie that Michael had come into my room, to which he merely replied, "Ssshhh! This IS his house - and you know how lucky we are to be able to stay" he added.

My foster parents WERE right.

I WAS an ungrateful little bastard who didn't appreciate anything anyone did for me. Michael had given me a home when I needed one and I couldn't even keep my mouth shut for one minute without moaning because he wanted to screw me. Who did I think I was anyway?

I was a kid with no real parents and Jim and Enid had taken me and Beverly in as their own.

Even the social workers had been sick of me moaning about how bad my life was. I'd tried to tell them about the beatings once, because that's what Childline had told me to do when I had phoned them from a phone box when I was eleven. Childline was a free phone service for abused kids. I'd seen the advert a thousand times on television and memorized the number, so, on my way to school one day, after being on the receiving end of the leather belt the night before, for God only knows which one of many reasons, I decided to phone Childline to tell them.

They asked me lots of questions and I desperately wanted to answer them all, but I was so scared that I would open a can of worms, only for nothing to happen, and then I would have to face Jim when the police had gone. Either way, I would be doomed.

They couldn't promise me that he would be taken away, so, I had to listen to their only other advice which was for me to tell my social worker the next time she would visit.

I kept an eye on the bruising for the next few days to make sure that it was still there to show my social worker.

He arrived for the usual fortnightly visit and I felt sick to the pit of my stomach with nerves. Beverly went in to see him first then, after she was finished, it was my turn.

I was about to pull my trousers down but, before I had the chance to undo my belt, I was interrupted.

Shit! It was Enid coming in. She had overheard Beverly and I discussing what I was going to say to the social worker when he arrived. After I had gone into the room she had quizzed Beverly, and, being scared of the repercussions, she had told her that I was going to speak to the social worker about getting the leather belt. Before I knew it, she was in the room telling him that I had been 'smacked' last night for being bad and that I had a 'small' mark on my leg.

The social worker just shook his head from side to side saying, " I wish you realised how lucky you both were for having a caring mum and dad"

I couldn't believe it! My chance to tell all was ruined, completely, now. Here I was faced with a man, who only visited once every two weeks, telling me that I was 'LUCKY!' before launching into a lecture about the boy who had cried wolf. I told him that it had been a belt and not a hand that had slapped me.

Enid glared at me and then heaved a long sigh, "See what I mean, Nigel?"

"Yes" the social worker replied "A bit of an overactive imagination".

I couldn't believe it.

I was trapped then and I was trapped now.

That very next day Jamie sat me down to tell me that he'd had word that his girlfriend had seen something on the television about me running away and that she had called the police to tell them where I was.

"Bitch!" I muttered through gritted teeth. I thought she had liked me. What had I done to her for her to go and, purposefully, try and get me caught?

She knew why I'd run away. It just didn't add up.

"How did you find out?" I asked. Jamie became a little jumpy.

"She phoned here last night when you were asleep," he said.

"Anyway, the thing is, the police are going to come looking for you so we need to move on quickly," he added.

In later years, I was to find out that no phone call had ever been made. Donna had liked me after all.

Where will we go?" I asked in a panic-stricken voice.

I was completely unaware of what was going on.

"Michael is going to visit some friends in Liverpool and he reckons that there is a spare flat lying empty that we can use for the next two weeks until the heat has died down; then we can come back here," Jamie answered.

"Well, at least it stops me getting caught," I said. I couldn't go back now, not even if I'd wanted to. I'd been away too long now. I might have to be screwed every day, but at least I was wanted by men who could look after me and didn't hit me.

The next day we all got ready to set off to Liverpool.

"Does it take long to get there?" I asked Michael.

He started to laugh.

"What?" I was inquisitive.

"Only about EIGHT HOURS!" he replied, still laughing.

"EIGHT HOURS!" I exclaimed in pure disbelief.

That was a lifetime.

I don't remember what we talked about for most of the journey but I remember by now, feeling at complete ease in the back of the car and leaning forward most of the way just in case I missed any of the conversation that Michael and Jamie might be having. I didn't feel at all in danger. I was actually looking forward to the change of scenery. Indeed, I felt like I was going on holiday.

After an hour or so on the road, Michael suggested that we stop off at the next service station for some food. I was pleased to hear him say that, as I was starving!

We all had a huge, fried, all-day breakfast, which went down a pure treat.

After we had finished, we filled the car up with petrol and Michael asked whether or not I would like some sweets from the garage.

"Please!" I said excitedly. I had a really sweet tooth.

Michael was away for a few minutes paying for the petrol and on his return he threw a large white paper bag into the back of the car.

Excitedly I ripped open the bag to peer inside. There was a carton of

Ribena - I loved Ribena! - and a bag of Maltesers, another of my favourites.

Then, the last bag caused all that excitement to drain from every part of my body. I began to shiver.

"What's happening to me? I feel sick and sweaty, yet I shiver like I'm cold."

Blackout.

I was having a flashback.

Suddenly, I found myself sitting watching the Saturday morning trash

T.V when I heard our names being shouted.

"Leon….Beverly….get through here!" shouted Jim from the kitchen.

What did he want now?

We got up quickly and went through to the kitchen where he was standing over the kitchen chair.

"Right then. Who's first?"

I was confused. First for what? And why was the kitchen chair out?

"Oh no. What now" I said silently in my head where no- one could get in.

"Don't look so confused, Leon. You know what this is about" he said, smirking.

"I don't…. honestly I don't" I replied. I was already shaking at this point because I knew these games only too well. We were about to be accused of something. I genuinely didn't know of what this time.

There had been times in the past when I had been guilty of 'theft' from the pantry and had been leathered with the belt, but I could almost handle that kind of abuse because I knew I'd 'stolen' from my parents and had to be punished for it.

My mind was all over the place by this point. Beverly looked at me with such fear. I knew by that look that she knew what this was about. He opened the cutlery drawer and took out HIS bag of strawberry-flavoured Bonbons. We knew we weren't allowed to touch them, and if we did, then we knew there would be huge repercussions.

"There are two sweets missing out of this bag," he said staring at the two of us, his eyes darting from one to the other.

He looked at Beverly and asked her where the sweets had gone. She said she didn't know.

Then he looked straight at me and asked me the same question.

"I haven't taken them," I said with my voice becoming shaky.

"Don't tell lies, Leon. I can tell it was you. Look at your face," he said in that whining voice.

But I knew for a fact I hadn't done it. This time I also knew he wasn't playing one of his twisted games - for two reasons.

The first reason was that Beverly's face had said it all. Why wouldn't she just admit it? We were on the verge of getting another beating and she was willing to carry on lying.

The second reason that I knew he wasn't making it up was because, usually, if he'd made it up, he would get pleasure out of belting us, but he didn't do that this time.

"Right then. I don't want thieving little bastards living in this house with me. Go on," he said pushing us into the back door.

"Fuck off out there; that's where scum goes, out next to the rubbish" he added forcefully pushing us outside.

"It's pouring down" I cried. We still had our pyjamas on.

'SMACK!' He struck the back of my head with the left over bag of bonbons, screaming, "Just get out and don't be so fucking cheeky!".

We both started to cry as he locked the door behind us.

How long would we be out there for? He was capable of anything. He could leave us to die out here if he really wanted to. We stood there shivering in the cold; our pyjamas were completely wet through now.

I looked up and in through the French windows of the living room which looked out into the yard where we stood.

"Turn around and face the other way," he shouted through them.

We turned to face the opposite way, tears rolling down our cold cheeks.

"That's better," he yelled, "I can't stand looking at thieving twats!"

Here we were again: made to feel like pieces of scum. Put out with the trash. Filthy orphans.

Blackout.

I was back in the car: safe. I was away from Jim.

"Leon…are you ok?" asked Jamie.

I told my 'other' me that having to lie and be raped wasn't half as painful as having my mind destroyed.

It was from that moment on that I realised that giving men what they wanted could make my world a better place to be.

"Leon, are you all right" he asked again. "Yeah. I was just remembering a bad memory," I replied.

"Well, just remember that we are here to look after you now".

I weighed up my options and knew that Jamie was right.

"I'll give them what they want. It's only sex. They can't destroy me by taking that, can they? At least they don't want my mind. That's more important. As long as I have my 'other' me, I will survive."

After remembering the Bon-Bon incident, my mind went into overdrive to remind me once more, that I was in safer hands here.

One of Jim's favourite games was to catch us off guard just when we thought everything was o.k. He would hunt for clues, anything to find us having done something wrong, looking around the house like a wild animal scavenging for food.

On one of these occasions Jim said that I had been caught out by the 'Devil's Clues'. That's what he called the evidence that would catch us.

It was another of the school holidays and I was nine, maybe ten. Enid was working full- time in a nursing home and Jim was at the farm. He would come home at lunchtime to check that we were still in the house and not getting into any trouble.

On one of these afternoons, in the holiday, Beverly and I had decided to make up some Angel Delight. It was strawberry flavour: our favourite.

We had both decided that if we took the dessert and made it up, ate it and cleared up before anyone got home, then, who would even know?

That afternoon, we happily messed around in the kitchen and made up the dessert. It seemed to take ages to set properly but, after about an hour in the fridge it was ready to eat. We gulped it all down within minutes. Quickly afterwards, we cleared everything away and spent the rest of the day watching T.V. That evening, Jim came in from work and ate his tea as normal. At nine 'o' clock we headed off to bed and I fell asleep quite quickly that night.

Suddenly, I heard a loud scream and, on opening my eyes, I saw Jim's face right up against mine, our noses touching.

"GET UP!" he screamed.

The sickness flooded my body as he flung back my bed covers and dragged me to my feet. 'SLAP!' He struck me right across the face with such force that I thought my neck was going to snap.

"Aarrgh! Plea…s..e," I whimpered.

"Ple…ase. Ple…ase," he mimicked as Enid watched on, having already dragged Beverly from her room in the same way.

He punched and slapped me - and Beverly - over and over until we both admitted what we had done.

"What do you say to your dad?" Enid said.

"Sorry. Sorry for stealing from you," Beverly and I both said at the same time.

Yet again we had proved to be worthless pieces of shit.

We were orphans who had been given a chance in life and then repaid their saviours by 'stealing' from them.

"What did we do wrong?" Jim would ask.

"You never did anything wrong. It's us," we would reply to them, having rehearsed the line a thousand times. That was one of their mind games, you see. They would blame themselves for us turning out the way we had, so that we would then tell them that we were the ones to blame and not them.

Maybe they were right after all.

This frame of mind would stay with me for years to come: self-loathing, self-hating and despising my very own existence.

How did he know about the dessert anyway? No sooner had I asked myself this question, than the answer was delivered.

"Devil's clues always catch the evil ones in the end," he said calmly, rubbing the red mark from his hand from where he had struck the same piece of skin time after time when he'd punched and slapped us.

What we didn't realise at that point was that Jim always counted the food in all of the cupboards, so that he would know if we had been 'stealing' the biscuits or any other source of food other than what we were given at meal times. Eating between meals was classed as 'greed' and 'gluttony' as they would often preach to us, while chewing on an apple between meals, because, you see, they were adults.

"Adults need more food than kids," they would add while scoffing it down.

"I wasn't even going to count the food last night, until I found a bit of powder on the corner of the kitchen table," he said with a pleased look on his face.

Shit! I thought to myself. When we were making the dessert some of the powder had fallen onto the table and we hadn't noticed it. Jim had then come in from work and while he was eating his tea he had noticed the 'Devil's clue' and investigated further. He tasted the miniscule dash of powder and recognised the taste. Once he realized, he then investigated even further by counting the packets of Angel Delight. He knew all this before we had gone to bed, yet he had still sent us, knowing that we would get more of a fright by being dragged from our sleep.

It was just another way to try and break us.

I was enjoying this long, car journey with Michael and Jamie.

"Where are we staying?" I asked Michael.

"I have a spare flat in a place called Magna, it's just outside Liverpool. You'll be safer there," he said in his usual tone of kindness. If I hadn't known better, I would have thought that the incident with him the other night hadn't happened at all. He never acted any differently with me and it was as if I had imagined the whole thing; but the physical pain, which remained, served to remind me that it was all too real and had, indeed, happened.

I drifted in and out of a deep sleep and, not before long, we had arrived at Magna.

"You two wait here in the car while I go and get the keys from Alan."

Michael said as he stepped out of the car.

We waited no longer than ten minutes until Michael arrived back, waving the keys at us.

"Come on then!" he said excitedly.

I was just as excited. It really did feel like a holiday: a holiday with people who truly loved me. I was so lucky.

We all ran for the door.

"Last one in has to make the tea," shouted Jamie.

"That's not fair," I shrieked "I've got shorter legs than you two," I added, running and laughing at the same time. I was soon gasping for breath.

Once we were inside, Michael showed me round the flat, but Jamie said that he didn't need to look round as he'd seen it before. I thought it strange that he hadn't mentioned that he had already been here.

I wandered around the flat and Michael pointed out which would be his bedroom and that the other bedroom would be for Jamie and me to share.

My heart lifted when he took me in and there was a double bed staring back.

I was going to be cuddled tonight. I was also going to have Jamie inside me first thing in the morning, but then I reminded myself that anything was better than going back to Jim Frazer.

I opened my eyes and, for a split second, I didn't realise where I was, waking up in my new surroundings. I turned round to see why Jamie hadn't woken me, but he wasn't there. Where was he? Quickly, I jumped up in a panic.

What if they've brought me here and just left me? Had they wanted rid of me?

I darted for the bedroom door and ran into the front room.

"What the hell is wrong with you?" Jamie shouted.

I'd given him a shock when I'd run through into the room. He was sitting in silence, drinking a glass of orange juice.

"I wondered where you were," I said, a little embarrassed.

"Just enjoying some quiet. Go back to bed," he retorted.

I knew something was wrong with him, but I didn't know what; I went back to bed and lay there, for what seemed like hours, waiting for him to come in and do his usual to me. I waited and waited, but still he didn't appear. Had I done something wrong?

Why didn't he want to touch me anymore? Did he not love me anymore? Had I pissed him off like I had with everyone else in my life so far? I didn't know.

Just then, while deep in thought, the door began to slowly move. The door creaked as it crept open. A face peered around the corner. Who was that?

"Ow ya doin', mate?" asked the stranger, in a very broad Geordie accent.

"Who are you?" I quizzed, albeit nervously, pulling the bed covers up to my chin.

"Ma name's Jim, mate….are YOU Leon?" he asked.

"Er….yer" I said wondering what he was doing here.

"Is that dirty sod leaving you alone?" he said smiling.

"Who?" I asked.

Just then, Jamie shouted from the other room.

"Jim, leave him alone…he's sleeping"

"Calm ya sel down, man…I'm only chatting ti'im" he shouted back to

Jamie.

"Isn't that right mate?" he said looking at me.

"Yeah. I'm fine," I shouted through to the other room.

No sooner had I finished saying I was fine than Jamie came bolting through to where I was lying and growled at me that I'd better stop showing off in front of Jim.

I couldn't believe it. I hadn't done anything! The only thing I had been doing was to wait in the bed, like a good boy, waiting for him to come and rape me.

"Keep your eyes off …He's MINE," he hissed at Jim.

"Calm ya sel down man…I was just introducing ma sel," Jim spat back.

Jamie then looked back at me and told me it was time to get out of bed.

As soon as they both had left the room, I started getting ready as quickly as I could. Then the door creaked open again. It was Jamie.

"Don't make a fool out of me…are you listening?" he said in a semi-loud whisper.

"I didn't do anything….I was waiting for you to come back to bed and then he came into the room" I said protesting my innocence.

"Oh! So it's my fault," he snapped back.

He slowly walked over to the bed where I was sitting, putting on a pair of socks. I started to feel scared at this point because he looked different. He looked really angry. I'd seen that kind of look on a face before: Jim Frazer's face.

What was he going to do? I really hadn't tried to make a fool of him.

As he was walking over to the bed one of his arms reached out towards me. What was he going to do!

"Please don't hurt me, Jamie," I begged.

He was getting closer and closer by the second.

"Jamie, you're scaring me," I whispered, so as not to let anyone else hear, because I knew that would make this situation worse.

He reached out for me, touching my neck with the tip end of his longest finger and pushed it against my Adam's apple.

"Please…." I whispered.

His eyes widened and seemed to become more and more bloodshot before my very eyes.

His whole hand tightened around my throat. I was gasping for breath.

I told my 'other' me that this was just a joke. It had to be, I hadn't done anything.

I felt the blood rushing to my head as my face tightened really quickly.

He began to speak in a strange voice that he was putting on. It almost sounded like Darth Vader from the *Star Wars* movie.

What was he doing this for?

"You're mine…Do you hear….Mine…I don't want you…No-one else is ever having you though… No-one!" he said in the scary voice.

My face was growing tighter and tighter. I thought he was going to strangle me until I stopped breathing.

Suddenly, he stopped and began to laugh heartily.

"You should have seen your face…. ! What a picture!" he said getting up.

I held my throat. The pain was incredible! It felt like he had pushed my Adam's apple into the back of my throat. He went to stroke my head and I flinched.

"Come on…don't be like that… I was only messing on," he said smiling.

Jamie then turned and left the room, still laughing and shaking his head.

What the hell was going on with him?

From that moment on, I was terrified of him and didn't want to be left alone with him for a single minute.

I finished getting dressed and then made my way into the living room where Michael, Jamie and Jim were sitting. I couldn't even look at Jamie after what he had just done.

"Is he shagging you?" Jim asked looking at me.

Jamie interrupted.

"Shut up, eh! He's just a pal, isn't that right, Leon?" he said staring at me.

Well he had just told me he didn't want me anymore, so I suppose he wasn't lying.

"Yeah…just pals," I replied, in a half croaking voice, having just been almost strangled to death by my 'pal'!

"D'ya fancy a shag?" Jim said to me with a huge grin on his face.

I must have looked shocked.

"He's kidding on with you," laughed Michael, then turning to Jim and saying "Isn't that right, Jim!"

"Aye man, I was joking on…I'm married with kids me," he answered with the huge grin still on his face.

We all started to laugh.

I had immediately taken to Jim; he was a proper cocky Geordie lad with blonde hair and, against me, he looked about six foot tall. He wasn't muscular like Jamie, he had a more toned physique. They were chatting about a place called Geppo's bar, which was in central Liverpool - and discussing how they could get me in to the nightclub afterwards. I was only fourteen after all, although I looked and passed for much older. I'd been served cigarettes since I was twelve years of age. Beverly was two years older than me yet they wouldn't serve her cigarettes at the local newsagents, so that became my 'job' on the way to school.

Jim mentioned that he knew the owner of the nightclub and that it would be cool to get in.

Could I believe what I was hearing? I was going out to a 'grown-up' pub? Then, to top it all off, a nightclub?

That was the plan then. Michael would take me into town and treat me to some new clothes to go out and then we would head for Liverpool, from Jim's house, around eight o' clock. Jim also mentioned that we could stay at his home, afterwards. I was really excited now. I'd quickly forgotten about what had happened not but twenty minutes earlier with Jamie, although I had decided that I didn't want to lie next to him anymore; but then, in my situation, what choice did I have?

"Come on then" Michael said rubbing his hands "Let's get you some nice clothes to go out in"

"I'm dead excited about tonight…I've never been out before," I said, in complete awe of the situation.

"It'll be a good night…you'll love it," he replied.

We headed off into town and were soon weighed down with bags from Burtons. I'd never had 'designer' clothes before. I thought to myself," If Jim and Enid could see me now, eh." I'd always been dressed with hand-me-down clothes or stuff from that crap shop in Canton called 'Danny's Discounts'. That was another reason for why I'd been bullied at school. I was always sent there in what could only be described as fashion from seven seasons ago. Which is why, to this day, I have an obsession with good, trendy clothes.

When I'd started my second secondary school I had needed some new shoes. Of course I dreamt of having a pair of shoes like the boy band 'Bros' but Jim and Enid had other ideas in mind. After walking for hours on end into all the fancy shops in Canton town centre and Enid purchasing another pair of £200 sandals - as she did every other weekend and Jim took his turn on the alternate weekends, -we headed to 'Danny's'.

"You two need to realise that we can't afford to buy you expensive shoes and clothes," he said.

"We're not made of money, you know," she said.

After which, he finished with the usual put down line of "If it wasn't for us then you wouldn't have a home... never mind having any clothes"

I hated living like this. Why did they always make us feel so shit about ourselves? We knew we were different. We were told often enough so as never to forget.

We started looking at the shoes when Jim spotted a box full of black boots.

"These ones will do him," he said picking up a boot and showing Enid.

I looked up in horror.

"They're girl's boots," I said, beginning to cry. I knew they wouldn't listen once they had decided what was suitable. Even the shop assistant looked at me with pity.

"The foster kids need new shoes," Jim said smiling at the woman.

Straight away her face changed from a look of pity to a look as if to say we should be lucky we were getting anything from people who weren't our parents.

So there I was, holding a bag of girl's £6 boots for my new term at school.

I was dreading the first day back at school with those horrible boots. I just wanted to be normal like all the other lads. All right, so maybe I didn't have real parents, but at least I could feel half normal by wearing boy's boots and not girl's ones.

On my way out of the door I took a sneaky look at myself in the mirror.

We weren't allowed to stand at the mirror because, according to Jim and

Enid, it would make us love ourselves.

My hair was sticking up so I decided to run upstairs and wet it in the hope that it would flatten it down. I knew the rules. No wetting hair, no hair gel and no looking in the mirror, apart from when you brush your teeth.

"Who the fuck do you think you are?" snarled Enid.

"What?" I said pretending to not know what she was talking about.

"Don't 'what' me… Get up them stairs and get that dried…NOW!" she screamed.

Just as I was half way up the stairs she screamed again.

"Get back here"

What was it now?

She grabbed me by the chin and twisted my face towards hers.

"Where did all those spots come from?" she asked accusingly.

"I don't know…they just keep appearing," I said, not understanding what she was getting at.

"LIAR!" she screamed.

'SMACK!' She hit me full force across the face.

"What was that for?" I asked with tears running out of my eyes like a tap.

"You've been bloody glue sniffing haven't you?" she replied.

"What…? They're spots…everyone has them…I haven't done anything," I protested.

Yet again I was trying to fight a losing battle.

I was trying to protest my innocence.

"Just get out of my sight," she said shaking her head in disgust at me.

After drying my hair, and crying more tears, I headed off to catch the school bus.

When I arrived at school, assembly time was about to start. Fortunately, we had to take our shoes off for assembly, so at least that was one saving grace not having the embarrassment of walking into the whole of the school population wearing girl's boots. Once it had finished, however, we all left the hall and into the corridor to collect our shoes. As I bent down to put mine on someone shouted.

"POOF!" echoed up the long corridor.

There was a silence for a split second and then, all of a sudden, a stampede of the older lads ran past, punching me and spitting at me. I lost my balance and fell down the corridor stairs. All the other people in my class just kept walking because they didn't want to get involved.

I hated my life!

For the rest of the day, I dragged my feet up and down the playground to wreck these cheap and nasty shoes. I knew I would be punished for ruining them, but I didn't care.

Michael and I were heading back to the flat from our shopping trip when he said we should pop in and see Jim to finalise times and plans for the night out.

We arrived at a house, which was in the middle of a large block.

Michael knocked at the door and a little girl came to the door.

"Is your Dad in?" asked Michael.

I thought Jim had been kidding when he said he had a wife and kids.

"DADDY...Uncle Michael's at the door," she screamed at the top of her voice.

"Come in!" shouted Jim from inside the house.

We went into the house and were greeted by a matronly-looking woman called Julie, who turned out to be Jim's wife. She was really nice.

Next, I was introduced to their daughter, Emma, who had answered the door. Also living in the house with them was their newborn, called Aaron, and

Jim's Uncle Alan. I remember thinking what a loving, warm feeling I sensed from entering this house.

"Let's see your stuff then," said Jim.

I went into the kitchen and put on my new clothes. I had chosen a new shirt with a blue paisley pattern running along the collar and cuffs - believe it or not that was the height of fashion then - a new pair of dark jeans and some new tan shoes. I remember feeling like a pop star when I walked back through into the living room where they were all sitting.

"Oooooooooh!" they all exclaimed, as I paraded up and down the room.

I felt amazing.

"Do you want a cuppa?" Jim asked us both.

"No thanks…we better get going, to head back up to the flat" answered

Michael. I must admit to being a little disappointed. I could quite easily have stayed there for a lot longer. Besides which, it was a breathing space away from Jamie.

After saying our goodbyes, we headed back to the flat to get ready for going out later. Jim had decided that he would come and meet us up at the flat at eight instead of us going to his place, as he didn't want Julie to know where we were going.

Obviously, she didn't know that her husband wasn't completely straight.

He had the chance to escape and "be gay" for the night, whenever Michael visited them from London.

It reached about six 'o' clock and I couldn't contain myself any longer. I just had to start getting ready! I went into the bathroom and started running a bath when I sensed someone behind me. I turned around quickly. It was Jamie. He came up behind me and pressed his body against me, I could feel his penis pressing hard behind me; he said he wanted me to go into the bedroom.

I knew exactly what he wanted to do with me. He wanted to use my body as a plaything and then discard me like a piece of rubbish once he'd shot his load inside me.

"I'm getting ready," I said, laughing the suggestion off.

"I'm not asking for permission," he said, with a smirk on his face.

Here I go again. Lie down, groan and act as if I'm getting pleasure from a muscular, fifteen stone, good-looking guy who has turned out to be nothing more than a bully and an abuser.

I closed my eyes and winced in pain as he pushed himself deep inside me without the use of lubrication. While my eyes were closed he couldn't see me cry or see the pain that I felt as he rammed in and out, faster than a sowing machine stabbing through fresh cloth. He groaned as he emptied his sacks of cum deep inside me, then, without warning he pulled out…

"That was good," I said, with half open eyes.

"Try and act like you're fucking enjoying it next time then," he retorted as he wiped himself on a towel.

"I did," I lied.

"Go and get ready for the night out" he ordered.

He knew that I was lying. It was so difficult, though, to pretend I was getting pleasure from him, when I was so scared.

After cleaning away the residue he had left on me, I wandered through to the bathroom, where I had been not more than five minutes earlier to have a bath. Jamie switched on the Hi-fi in the living room and high-energy music blasted into every room. I was still so excited about tonight. I couldn't wait to see Jim!

"I wonder if he will want to touch me?"

Just at that the door buzzer went.

"'Ow yous doing?" said the voice in the corridor.

That Geordie accent was very familiar.

Jim had arrived and I had butterflies flying around my stomach!

"How ya doin, sexy," Jim said, squeezing my bum and winking as he brushed past me. My heart raced as the blood flushed through my brain at what seemed like a hundred miles an hour. I felt my face getting hotter and hotter, to the point of nearly exploding!

"Oh, my God!" I said to my 'other' me. I really fancy him! He'll look after me and keep me safe from harm, guarding me from danger and evil.

So many thoughts raced through my head.

Is this what being in love means? Does this mean I'm a full-blown gay?

I had never, ever felt what I was feeling at that very moment. The very thought of him made my stomach do somersaults. My heart would race when he looked at me. I would blush like one of those sun-blushed tomatoes that you buy in the shops for "posh" salads. When he brushed past me, every hair on my body would stand on end, shivers and tickly feelings running up and down my back, from my feet to my head and back again. Just one look from him would make me feel amazingly warm.

How could this be? I had known him for only a day.

What was happening to me?

Just then, my thoughts were disrupted. I was distracted by a large clinking sound. It was Michael. He was walking through from the kitchen with a tray, full of glasses, filled with what looked like apple juice. He placed them down on the coffee table in the living room.

"What's that?" I asked inquisitively.

"Don't tell me you've never had cider," he answered smiling.

"No, what is it?" I said, oblivious to the fact that cider was a well-known alcoholic drink.

"You're definitely going to have a good night tonight!" answered Michael.

He gave us all a glass of the yellow fizzy liquid. I smelt the glass. It had a sweet smell, like the smell of apples. I took a sip.

"Well mate. What d'ya think? Nice stuff eh!" Jim said smiling at me.

"Yeah" I answered gulping down more.

"Hey, slow down," said Michael as he moved my arm that was holding the glass away from my mouth.

"Why?" I asked in an innocent voice.

"Cause you'll end up pissed!" said Jamie smiling. They all roared with laughter.

That glass of cider was the beginning of the end for me. My head began to feel light very quickly. I remember feeling like a huge grin had been painted on my face for the rest of the night. I felt so relaxed after that. The alcohol took away all my feelings of fear towards Jamie. I actually became quite cheeky with him towards the end of the night; but only because Jim was "egging me on" and winding the situation up.

Drunk on half a pint of cider! Anyone who knows me today would laugh at the thought of that. These days I usually drink everyone else under the table!

The taxi arrived outside the flat. This was it! We were going to the bright lights of the city for a night to remember. I rushed to the front door in absolute excitement. I still felt quite dizzy from the cider, but I didn't let that stop me. I really wanted to sit next to Jim in the taxi, so I rushed for the back door and hoped Jamie would get in the front.

He did!

Jim and Michael climbed in the back, with me in the middle. We'd been in the taxi for about ten minutes when Jim's hand started to brush up and down the side of my leg. He was to my left and Michael to my right. No-one else in the taxi was aware of what was happening at first but, after a few minutes, Michael cottoned on to what was going on. He looked over and smiled at me, then winked at Jim. We both smiled back. If Jamie had known what Jim was doing he wouldn't be happy, to say the least.

Jim touching me was arousing my body in a way that I had never experienced before. I remember that I kept looking at his lips, wondering what it would feel like to kiss him: his lips pressing against mine; the smell of his aftershave as he is rubbing against the side of my face; his stubble burning my soft skin; his hands squeezing the back of my head lovingly as the gentle force pressed our lips closer and closer together.

As we drew nearer to Liverpool, Jim's flirting reached fever pitch.

"I want you," he whispered into my ear as he pressed his hand on the side of my leg. I so desperately wanted him to want me.

"O.K mate, that's you here," the taxi driver announced.

"We're here?" I asked Michael excitedly.

"Yeah, that's us" he replied with a warm smile on his face.

It's funny you know, to this day I still don't feel any hate towards Michael even though he had sex with me that night in his flat. He never touched me again. It only ever happened that once.

"Come on, kid...out ya get" said Jim as he grabbed my left arm yanking me from the inside of the taxi.

We had been dropped off outside a bar called Geppo's Bar. I was so nervous again. A mixture of excitement and anticipation swept through my body at such a speed.

"What if I don't get in?" I said, with sheer panic in my voice.

"You'll be fine. Just keep calm and don't bring attention to yourself", Michael replied.

Was he kidding! I was a fourteen year old, blond boy who was trying to pull himself off as twenty-one year old!

We walked up the steep staircase, in single file, until we reached a large, badly-lit room. Across the other side of this room was a bar with a large guy propped up behind it. Michael told me to sit with Jim in one of the booths that was right beside us, as he and Jamie would go to the bar. I had no qualms about staying there as it gave me the chance to be alone with Jim for the first time.

"I totally fancy you, mate," Jim said in his deep, manly voice. I loved the way he talked, especially with that thick, Geordie accent. I didn't know what to say and felt so stupid that I was given this chance to be alone with him for only a few minutes and all I could manage for an answer was a giggle and a bright red face. I couldn't help it. Whenever he spoke to me, my face would flare up.

"D'ya wanna stay wid me tonight?" he asked looking into my eyes.

"Erm…ye…yeah," I spluttered.

He smiled at me with such a sparkle in his eyes.

Michael and Jamie came back to the table with some drinks.

"Is that more cider?" I asked.

"Sure is…. but take it slower this time!" Jamie replied in an unusually calm voice. He was being genuinely friendly.

"Geppo's coming over in a minute or two. It's fine though, I've told him about Leon. He says he'll turn a blind eye," Michael said to Jim.

"Nice one, mate." Jim replied.

Just then I saw, what looked like a rather large woman, with make up plastered all over her face like a clown, coming towards us. She came right over to the table and leaned against it to give everyone a kiss on both cheeks.

"And you must be the chicken!" she said looking at me.

She sounded just like a man. I mean, like a proper man.

The shock must have been written all over my face when she spoke, because they all started to laugh.

"My name's Leon." I answered in a confused state.

I didn't understand what they all found so funny. What was a chicken, anyway?

After a couple of minutes, Geppo turned to leave.

"Have a great night, lads; and don't worry about the club, I'll give the manager, Gerry, a bell and let him know you're on your way," she said as she left.

"What do you think then…..? Of Geppo?" asked Michael.

"She seems really nice," I answered in an apprehensive voice. To be honest I was a bit confused.

They all laughed.

"Why do you all keep laughing?" I asked.

"Well, we could tell by your face that you were surprised when Geppo spoke," said Jamie.

"Was it because she sounded a bit manly?" added Jim.

"Probably," I answered.

"That's because she's a transsexual," he answered chuckling.

"What's that?" I asked innocently.

"A man dressed as a woman," answered Michael.

"You're joking!" I gasped in pure disbelief.

"No, really" answered Jim.

I was shocked! I knew there was something strange about her, but didn't think for one minute it was a man!

Then my next question was about the chicken comment.

"And what did she…he…Geppo mean when he called me a chicken?" I asked, directing the question at Michael.

"It's what they call young guys like you. It's another word for a young lad, that's all."

"Oh" I answered. I needed to drink a bit more cider, as the effects of the glass I'd had in the flat were beginning to wear off and I was starting to develop a headache.

"We'll have this one and then head off to the club, then, eh?" Jim said looking at us all.

Just then, I noticed someone staring at me from across the room. He was a very attractive, tall and dark-haired guy and he kept tilting his head to the side as if to tell me to go over. I froze on the spot. What did he want me to do? I wasn't sure.

He kept smiling at me, then tilting his head again. After nodding, he disappeared into the men's toilets. He was away for ages and then he reappeared. As soon as he was back to his standing place he began nodding again. He wanted me to follow him into the men's toilets. My heart was racing. I was trying really hard not to let the rest of them see me smiling at him. Although I was a "free agent", I worried I would upset

Jim.

"What do I do? What do I do?" I asked my 'other' me. I wasn't sure how to play this. Here I am in a bar with three men, two of whom had raped me at separate times over the last couple of weeks and the other who I knew I fancied like mad, but was married with two kids. Now, I'm being eyed up by a gorgeous guy in the corner beckoning me to the toilets. I made up my mind. I was going to follow him. .

" Just going to the toilet," I announced.

My heart really was racing as I made my way to the door.

What do I do when I get in there? I thought to myself.

Slowly, I walked through the door and there he was, standing there, waiting for me to go over.

"Oh my God!" I whispered to myself, through tight lips, as I walked towards him. He looked so sexy standing there. I moved closer.

"Hi!" I said, in a shy manner.

"Sssshhh…." he whispered as he put his index finger up to his lips.

He moved up towards me and ran a strong hand through my hair, putting his other hand on the side of my face and gently brushing my cheek with his thumb. Gently, he placed his index finger on his lips again as he moved himself closer towards mine. His finger still in place, touching my lips, I felt his warm sweet breath caress my skin as he moved it away. I was so caught up in the moment; and, although it was only minutes that we were together, each second seemed to pass in perfect slow motion. We kissed one another with such passion. What an amazing feeling to be wanted by a man! A feeling for which I would yearn over the next fifteen years.

"So what's your name?" he asked in a thick, Liverpool accent.

"Leon" I whispered.

" You are very sexy, Leon…My name's Jason by the way," he said, staring into my eyes. I never wanted this moment to end. It was perfect in every sense, even in the middle of the men's room!

"What ye doing tonight?" he asked.

"I'm going to a club with the guys out there, that I'm here with," I answered.

"Are you single?" he asked.

"I am, yeah," I answered.

"D'ya fancy coming to mine?" he said.

I didn't know what to say. I so desperately wanted to go with him, but I couldn't really. Without Michael and Jim, I was stuck. Thousands of things were racing through my mind at that very moment. How do I tell him why I can't go? ' Er….by the way….I'm a runaway kid from abusive foster parents'. I was stuck. Anyway I needed to remind myself that it was Jim I truly wanted, but was too scared to make a move on him. However, soon, I had a plan. I knew that couldn't burn my bridges at both ends, so I thought of a way to have the best of both worlds. I figured that if I arranged to meet Jason the following week then that would give me plenty of time to know what was going to happen with regard to where I was staying and with whom. If I was still in Liverpool, then I would know how things were going with Jim, because if nothing was to happen there, then I had made up my mind that I wouldn't be staying with Jamie, because God only knows what he would do to me. It was at this point that I realised how much I wanted to stay in the Liverpool area. I wasn't going back to London with Michael and Jamie.

Eventually, I answered his question:

"I can't… Not tonight anyway."

"'How come like?" he asked.

";Cause I'm out with that lot….Do you want to meet me here next Monday?" I asked him, as he stood smiling at me.

"Yer, 'course I do," he said in his thick accent.

"Twelve 'o' clock, then?" I suggested,

"Cool, I'll see you then," he replied.

At least this way I had more than one option. It was survival at the end of the day. I was learning, very quickly, that I would always need to be two - or even three - steps ahead to stay in the game.

No sooner had we finished making arrangements than the door swung open. It was Jim – and he was looking very annoyed.

"Jim…This is Jason…I was just talking to him," I said with obvious panic in my voice.

"What the fuck you up to, mate?" he asked, hissing at Jason.

"I'm just talking to the lad," Jason replied in a cocky voice.

"The boy's only fourteen, man…Go on…..Fuck off!" he shouted, as he pushed him out of the door.

I didn't think Jim was the type to get angry like that.

"Leon…You cannot just go off into the bogs and chat to strangers like that…Are you listening…? He could have been a nutter and fucking killed you!" he was shouting in an angry, yet caring way. I must have looked quite shaken because he then apologised and pulled me towards him.

"Do you like me or what?" he asked, staring right into my eyes.

I couldn't believe it! It was only a few minutes ago that I was wondering how I could tell him I liked him and here he was asking me the very question.

"Of course I like you!" I blurted out, as tears welled up in my eyes.

"What ya getting upset for?" he asked, in a very concerned way.

"Because I really like you! I want you to want me, Jim…. I know you're married and not properly gay but….," I blurted out, with tears now in full flow.

"But what…? Do you know something, Leon?" he said holding me so tightly.

"What?" I whispered.

"I don't even know ya and the feelings I'm feeling towards ya right now are crazy…. But I can't help it." Tears now welled up in his eyes.

This guy standing right in front of me was the most amazing man I had ever come across. That moment, right there, I knew I had fallen deeply in love with Jim.

Life would never be the same again and nor did I want it to be – because life without Jim wouldn't be a life worth living.

"Come on," he said ushering me out of the door.

We went back and joined the rest of the group. They were none the wiser as to what had happened in the toilets - and I don't think Jim ever did mention it to any of them.

Soon, it was time for us to hit the club. I'd drunk two more half- glasses of cider and was well on my way to becoming very drunk. We approached the club doors and, by now, with being in the fresh air, I felt even more away with it. I had to act completely sober now otherwise there was no chance I was going to get to see the inside of the club. My heart was racing with excitement as the high-energy music pumped out from behind the club doors and spewed onto the streets. I loved that type of music, it really got me going. I felt like some kind of pop star surrounded by bodyguards as I was shuffled into the club.

"If people at school could see me now, eh!" I thought" Fourteen years old, steaming drunk and heading into an over twenty-one's gay club."

As we walked up the dark hallway, I was mesmerised by the loud music leading me to the main part of the club. I remember a really strange smell in the air, as smoke from the smoke machine filled my lungs, my heart beginning to beat faster and faster, my body becoming lighter, my eyes turning to slits, a sense of total awe of what was in front of me. The interior glass doors swung open to reveal half-naked lads and men dancing in time to the music, as it blasted through the huge speakers on the floor, bodies making strange silhouette shapes on the backdrop of multi-coloured walls of light. This place was awesome, something I could never have dreamt up in my head; it pushed the boundaries of my imagination to the limit. Everyone hugging, kissing and caressing as the music grew louder and the smoke machine blew faster. Laser lights were bouncing off every part of the dancers' bodies. Above the speaker, a lad caressed his own body, rubbing himself, touching his chest with both hands, his fingers moulding into one and then, with a short flick, spreading out like the webbed feet of a duck as he continued to smooth over his body, touching his hips and sliding his hands down the front of his shorts, eyes closing in ecstasy.

My eyes were transfixed; they soaked up every bit of this atmosphere like a sponge. As I looked around, scanning the room through the smoke, my eyes were dazzled by the brightness of a light and, without warning, I was transported back to Kirkby Willows as if in some kind of time machine.

Suddenly, a sickness enters my stomach like a flood breaking down a wall.

It's too late, I'm already there.

Flashback.

Blackout.

Yesterday wasn't a good day. In fact it was pretty shit!

I was battered for doing something I didn't do. It was Beverly who 'stole' the jelly from the pantry the night before last. She told me when we got up yesterday morning what she'd done, but didn't know if anyone would have noticed it was missing, as it had been among other seven or eight packets of the stuff. Who was she kidding!

Sure enough, when we got down the stairs, her answer was waiting. Jim was standing, leaning against the kitchen table, with the Tupperware box containing the other jellies.

"Who was it?" he said, as he began to undo his belt from his trousers.

That usual feeling of nausea spread through me like a wild river. We were going to take it in turns to get the belt until one of us gave in and admitted which one of us it was who'd taken the food. After being smacked with the belt four times, I knew Beverly was feeling

more fragile than me today, so I took the blame, purely because I knew that, this time, a genuine 'crime' had taken place and it wasn't one of his sick twisted games where he just made up the 'crime' to get a kick from seeing us beg him for mercy. Whenever you were the one who admitted to the 'crime', as your punishment, you would receive the extra number of belts which the other person had been given; in addition to the ones you had already received. In total I received eight cracks of the belt, four before I admitted to anything and then an extra four for the ones Beverly had 'wrongfully' received. I knew that, another time, when the chips were down, Bev would do the same for me. She owed me one. Little did I realise that I would be calling in that favour as soon as I did. Not even twenty-four hours later, I was begging her to take the blame for a 'crime' of mine that was about to be brought to the surface.

Still sore from the previous day's beating, my legs were throbbing as we walked back down the hill. We had all been visiting a place called Talking Tarn. It was the name of a hill on which a pub sat at the top and was famously known for being the highest pub in Britain. We walked all the way to the top, had our photograph taken next to the sign, then we made our way back down again. It was decided that, after the drive home, that we would go to some caves at a place called Stenkrith.

The main reason for doing all these activities was due to the fact that our foster sister, Jane, was back home to get married to Keith. She had moved away to Chelmsford to be with him, although Keith was actually our foster mum's cousin, which would make him and Jane second cousins.

They had brought Jane's friend, Janette, with them to meet everyone, as she was going to be bridesmaid at the wedding.

To cut a long story short, Jim and Enid were "showing off" and playing their usual sickly-sweet ways in front of strangers, to lead them to believe that we were a normal, loving family who often went on excursions at the weekend, so, after Talking Tarn we headed off towards Stenkrith.

Beverly and I travelled in Jane and Keith's car, while Janette went with Jim and Enid. We had to drive through Kirkby Willows to get to Stenkrith and, as we were doing so, Jim pulled over to the side of our street. Keith, naturally, pulled over to see why we had stopped.

"How come we've stopped?" asked Keith as he wound down the window.

"I've just realised that we'll need the torch if we're going into the caves," he answered and then walked across the road towards the front door of our house.

Quicker than lightning my blood ran cold. The torch? The torch!

"Shit!" I said turning to Beverly in the back of the car. My eyes were wide with fear.

She realised something was horribly wrong, as the blood drained from my

face and I began to shake.

"What?" she whispered anxiously.

"The torch…I took the batteries out ages ago," I said, as my voice trembled.

"He won't realise," she said trying, quickly, to reassure me.

"I didn't put them back!" I said in sheer panic.

"Oh my God! Leon…. You idiot!" she answered as she now realized the trouble I was in.

"Please say it was you Bev…please…I'm still sore from yesterday…. My legs are all bruised," I said in terror.

At that point, out of the corner of my eye, I saw Jim hurtling across the road towards Keith's car waving the torch above his head like a crazed axe murderer. I was terrified!

"Pleeaassssssse" I hissed, as he got closer.

"All right…all right! I'll do it," she answered.

The car door swung open. He grabbed me by the collar and dragged me across the road and into the house, pushing me so hard that I fell, head first, onto the kitchen door. Blood gushed down the side of my face as I screamed in agony, begging for him not to hurt either of us.

"WAIT THERE!" he screamed, spit flying from his mouth into my face.

101

"Please God...Please don't let him hurt us" I prayed as he stormed outside to fetch Beverly from the back of the car. By this point she was cowering into the back seat like a scared animal. Blood trickled down my face.

"Please God" I whispered over and over as I heard him dragging Beverly up the hallway and heading for where I was standing. I hadn't seen him in this much of a rage for ages. He looked like a wild animal hunting for his prey.

Us.

He stood towering over us like a wild animal weighing up his options, weighing up what he could do to cause us as much distress as possible.

First, there was a deadly silence and then... THUMP!

"Aaarrgghhh!" I screamed, holding my head in pain as even more blood sprayed into the air.

"DAD! Please!" Beverly screamed in sheer terror at what she was witnessing. She didn't realise that my head was already cut so, to her, it looked a thousand times worse. His next punch hit Beverly's skin and, almost immediately, her face began to swell. Lashing out at us for what felt like an eternity, raining blows to our heads and faces again and again.

Silence.

"Where are they?" he said through seething teeth.

"What?" I asked, cowering away from his glare.

"Don't come the fucking innocent with me," he said, temper beginning to boil again.

"I don't know what you mean," I lied, praying that he wouldn't see through this deception.

"I'm not giving any chances to either of you this time, so I'm going to ask you once and once only. Where are the batteries from the torch?" he addressed us both. He then turned to me.

"Do you know where they are?" he asked calmly.

"No" I lied.

"Do you know where they are?" he asked again, turning to Beverly, knowing that she would have to say yes, otherwise we would be truly sorry this time.

"Yes," she whimpered.

"Where?" he demanded, never taking his eyes away from her fragile and terrified face.

She didn't respond.

"WHERE!" he screamed in her face.

She jumped in fear. I couldn't believe that I was making her take the blame for this. She would hate me.

"I...in...in my bedroom," she said stuttering.

No sooner had she finished her sentence than he grabbed her by the hair with such force that her heels lifted from the floor.

"Right then. We'd better get them," he said, dragging her up the hallway.

"Please" she begged.

The begging and pleading fell on deaf ears as he continued to drag her up the stairs. When they reached her bedroom, he threw her onto the bed.

"Are you going to show me where they are or will I look for them myself?" I heard him say, as I listened at the bottom of the stairs.

Suddenly something dawned on me.

"Shit!" I hissed to my 'other' me. How could she produce the batteries when she didn't even have them! She was covering for me. I had the batteries in my room. She couldn't possibly explain her way out of this.

The noise from the room was growing louder and louder as I heard him throwing things about in search for the batteries, his temper rising more and more by the second.

"Where the fuck are they?" I heard him scream.

"They're maybe in the cupboard under the stairs," Beverly cried out.

"Maybe! Fucking MAYBE!!! Either they are or they're not," he screamed back.

"They are," Beverly answered. She was so scared and it was my fault. It was one thing to "stick up" for one another, but this was different. This was so much worse. She didn't have a chance in this situation. It would be impossible. We both knew that he would never cave in: he would keep going and never tire of hurting us. He would carry on with this abuse until the batteries turned up. What could I do?

Just as I was about to run up the stairs to confess everything, Enid came bursting through the front door.

"What's going on? What have you done to make your Dad upset now?" she said, in an immediate attack on me.

No sooner had she spoken when Jim, still holding Beverly by the hair, came hurtling down the stairs.

"Out the road!" he screamed as he pushed past us.

"What's happened?" she asked.

"Why don't you ask this thieving little bastard!" he hissed twisting

Beverly's now limp body towards Enid.

"Well?" Enid demanded.

"I took the batteries out of the torch, but I can't remember where I put them," she answered.

"Then you'd better jog your memory and FAST!" Enid growled, her face only millimetres from Beverly's.

Jim dragged my sister to the cupboard under the stairs and swung the door open.

"Right! Where are they?" he demanded.

Beverly began to rifle through the tools in the cupboard, pretending to look for the batteries. Jim lost patience and, after pushing Beverly aside, he picked up the large yellow-handled screwdriver.

It all seemed to go in slow motion from that point.

He turned to Beverly who was cowering in the corner of the cupboard.

"You've lost them, haven't you?" he said accusingly.

"Yes," Beverly answered in defeat.

"You thieving BASTARD!" he screamed grabbing her by both arms.

She shook with terror as he forced her to place her hands face down on the small shelf.

"Have you any idea what happens to people who steal things in foreign countries?" he asked her.

Her face was blank. What was he going to do?

"They chop their thieving little hands off" he said. Beverly screamed as her brain began to tick. My eyes widened in disbelief! He couldn't chop her hands off! Could he?

Of course he could if he wanted to. He would probably enjoy it. But he was more clever than that. How would he get out of that one? His intentions became clear.

"Hold your hands out," he said calmly.

"Please don't hurt me!" Beverly begged.

"I don't want to hurt you, but you have to learn. I'm doing this for your benefit, to teach you right from wrong. That's what parents do," he said in a cold, unconcerned voice.

He lifted the screwdriver above his head.

"Nooooooooooo!" Beverly screamed.

The screwdriver sliced through the air like a knife and smashed onto her knuckles.

"Argghhh!" she screamed in pain.

Beverly slumped awkwardly into the corner of the cupboard.

"DON'T.... STEAL.... MY.... THINGS" he screamed at her, kicking her in the side of her stomach between words.

She lay there, staring into my eyes. I stared back into the blackness of the cupboard.

I lowered my head, staring at the floor. I was disgusted with myself. I didn't even have the courage to admit it was me, because I was so scared of this bully: this bully who was battering my sister to a pulp because of some batteries that were missing. I was paying for this anyway. Maybe not physically, but mentally I was breaking. To watch my sister being beaten, spat at, kicked and punched and not even having the courage to do or say anything about it.

"I bet even God hates me now as well."

He reached down and picked her up by her tee shirt, her body was limp and lifeless.

"Right, you two, back to the car" he said in a voice showing no concern.

Blackout....

"What do ya think?" said the familiar voice.

I was been prodded in the side gently.

"Leon?" the voice said with concern.

"Www...what's that?" I said as I snapped back into reality.

"Are ya all right?" asked Jim, now holding me around the hips.

"Yeah, it's amazing this place isn't it?" I answered.

"I thought you'd like it like" he replied, smiling.

This truly was an amazing place. I'd never even seen a nightclub on television. Although this place was full of people, laughing and shouting over the loud music, it felt so peaceful.

The rest of the time in the club flew past in a blur, as I drank even more cider. The lights came up as the music lowered. The end of the night already!

Where had all the time gone? I was so caught up in this different world that five hours had passed without me even noticing. I had to be helped into the taxi by Jim and Michael.

Someone was missing.

"Where's Jamie?" I slurred through my very dry mouth.

"Jamie met up with an old friend and is staying with him tonight; you'll see him tomorrow though," Michael answered.

I remember feeling more than happy with that answer. At least I wouldn't need to sleep with one eye open, worrying if I was going to be either strangled or raped. The taxi pulled up outside Jim's house. As I stepped out of the taxi, I fell to the kerb in a drunken blur. All of a sudden, I had the urge to be sick. My head was thumping; even my eyes couldn't focus. What was happening to me!

"Come on", Michael said as he picked me up from the pavement.

"Where are we going?" I asked, holding my head, as the pain was too unbearable to stand.

"Back to the flat. I think that's the best place for you tonight" he answered.

We were supposed to be staying at Jim's tonight. In all honesty, I didn't really care where I slept, as long as I could get rid of this thumping headache. Michael managed to get me back to the flat and made me drink what seemed like ten pints of coffee to try and sober me up! It did work quite well. I just wanted my bed. As I lay there, the room began to spin but, eventually, I drifted off into a deep sleep.

Blackout.

The pain was almost instant as I opened my eyes. This was, as I later found out in life, my first hangover. What a killer!

I felt terrible as I made my way through to the kitchen for a much-needed glass of water. When I opened the bedroom door, I saw two familiar faces: Jim and Michael. They both had enormous grins on their faces.

"Are you feeling rough, mate?" Jim asked, as he came over and ruffled my hair playfully.

"I feel like I'm gonna die!" I answered, still holding my head as the pain hadn't eased any. If anything it felt worse.

"You'll feel fine once you've eaten and drunk plenty of water," Michael said in a reassuring voice.

"I hope so," I answered.

"Why don't you come round to mine later, if you're feeling any better?"

Jim said.

"That would be great, Jim, if you don't mind keeping your eye on him," answered Michael.

Michael was going to spend a couple of days with an old friend who lived in the next town. He had been going to go the next day but, as there was still no sign of Jamie, he decided he would go a day early and would leave Jim with the keys to the flat.

I arranged with Jim that I would get myself sorted out at the flat, lock up and make my way to his house, just around the corner, later.

After spending most of the day in bed, I got up and had a bath, after which I felt a thousand times better! I locked up the flat and headed to Jim's for some tea.

When I knocked at the door Jim's wife, Julie, answered.

"Hiya, pet. Come in" she said with a beaming smile on her face.

She took my jacket and took me through to the living room where

Jim, the two kids and his Uncle Alan were sitting.

"Wey hey! The piss head has sobered up!" Jim playfully shouted.

I blushed whenever he spoke!

Emma came running over to me and leapt up as, instinctively, I put my arms out to catch her.

This was such a lovely house, full of lovely people: a dream family even.

I sat down and ate my tea, feeling like part of this family. I was so happy that night, hearing stories about anything and everything. I didn't even care that I didn't know the people in the stories; I just remember feeling at home. This was my first feeling of a true home.

"Why not stay here tonight, mate?" Jim said looking at me.

"W…ell…" I said as I looked at Julie to see her expression, not sure how to answer.

"You're more than welcome, pet," she said.

Great! I thought to myself. This felt too good to be true, and, it was about to get better.

"I'll go and make us some hot chocolate", Julie said as she got up and made her way into the kitchen.

"You can sleep down here with me," Jim said looking at me and winking.

"How?" I asked, with a full-blown blush.

"We take it in turns to watch Aaron down the stair on a night, so that we both get some proper sleep, " he said smiling.

"Right," I acknowledged, as my heart began to pound.

"Lucky it's my turn tonight eh?" he said as he stood up and brushed past my leg in a way that Alan couldn't see.

"I wonder if he wants to have sex with me?"

I was so nervous, but excited at the same time.

It grew later and later and I became more and more tired. So much so, that I began to nod off. Eventually, Julie stood up.

"I'm off to bed now. Alan, you get your arse off that chair and get yourself to bed as well. The lads need to get some sleep," she said frowning at Alan.

Alan must have been about ninety years' old, at the very least. His life involved just sitting in one of the large armchairs in the living room and chain-smoking from the minute he got up, to the minute he went to bed and, in between, he would watch over Emma when Jim and Julie were out. Apparently he would sit up all night, if he wasn't chased off to his bed. Julie and Alan headed out of the living room and Jim got up to follow them.

"I'll be back in ten minutes. I'm just saying 'night' to Julie," he said looking back from the living room door. Those 'ten minutes' turned out to be over an hour. I sat in there, in the living room, staring at the television wishing for Jim to walk back through the door. I was really nervous and had been feeling that way all night, even though I felt comfortable, too, and thought Julie was great. I knew that I just wanted to be on my own with Jim. We hadn't spoken about anything that had been said in the toilets, on the previous night, in Geppo's bar. I began to think that maybe I had misunderstood the whole situation. Maybe he didn't like me in that way. Maybe it was simply the case that I wanted him so much that I'd imagined the whole conversation. Or, maybe he did want me yesterday, but didn't want me now. Why would he? What was there to want from a little nobody like me anyway? My dad killed himself to escape me; my foster dad wouldn't care if I was dead, so what the hell would Jim want anything to do with me for?

As my mind ran into an overdrive of self-hatred, the door began to open.

It was Jim.

"You all right, kid?" he asked, as he walked through the living room door.

My stomach felt as though there were thousands of butterflies fluttering around inside it, all at once. This was the moment I'd been waiting for. Here we were, all alone: me - and Jim.

"Yeah" I answered nervously.

He walked across the living room and sat down on the sofa, neither of us taking our eyes off one another for a single moment.

I was shaking. Just then I felt his warm fingers as he brushed them over my bare arm. The hairs on my arm stood upright like a line of soldiers on the command of attention from their officer in charge; bumps began to form on my skin, spreading like a wild fire eating up the forest life with an unsatisfied hunger.

I looked into Jim's eyes. He was so beautiful. His eyes were as blue as the sky on a hot summer day, sparkling like the glimmer on the ocean when the sun caresses it.

" Is this love?"

"Leon," he said so softly.

"What?" I whispered back.

"Take off your tee shirt and sit down on the floor," he encouraged. I must have looked a little confused.

"It's o.k. Trust me, I'm not going to hurt you," he added. .

Just as he asked, I began to peel off my tee shirt as I slid off the sofa and on to the floor. He stayed sitting on the sofa as I faced away from him and rested my back against the sofa and in between his legs. I felt his warm breath against the back of my neck, as his hands gently gripped around my chest, his warm lips pressing against my ear as he whispered to me.

"I want to make love to you," he said gently.

My body began to relax as I became aroused by his tender words.

"Just relax; I want this to be the most amazing experience for you, to feel wanted and to feel needed. I want you, Leon," he said.

His words echoed around my head. Was I dreaming? How did he know me so well in such a short space of time? He wanted me. ME. I couldn't believe what was happening. This moment, right here, right now, in this room, just him and me on the verge of making love.

"Lie down," he whispered.

I did whatever he asked. Mesmerised by his words, I found myself unable to speak. I lay down on the floor with the support of his hands holding my head as he moved with me. His body was pressed tightly against me as he kissed me with such passion, my lips now stinging from his rough stubble. My body moved with such little effort. It seemed to become lighter and lighter, the more he touched me. With every touch of his hands, my body reacted and moulded into his skin. Slowly, he unbuttoned my jeans and slid them down over my thighs with such gentle care. He leaned above me taking off his shirt, slowly, then his jeans. Here we were as one, with only the light fabric of our underwear between us. He kissed and caressed my neck again but, this time he moved lower and then even lower as he placed his arm up and under my back, supporting it as it arched in response to his lips brushing over my stomach and then my navel. My hands seemed to become longer, my fingers endless as I glided them through my own hair and ran them over every strand. My mind became open, my fears banished, my heart lighter as I felt my soul connect to another human being. I began to remove my underwear as Jim removed his.

"I need to get some lube," he said gently.

I smiled adoringly at him.

It's so funny that no matter how much pain I'd had inflicted on me by so many people, it took just one moment of happiness and a feeling of self-worth to banish all of that pain. I truly believe that my survival, up until that point, was due almost entirely to a yearning for love. I would never give up the hope of experiencing this feeling, and so, whenever I met a person who showed me some kindness, I was immediately sold. To that day, in that room, lying there naked on Jim's living room floor, I was open to be loved and, until betrayal had occurred, I was solely that person's property.

My own paranoia would be a self-destructive weapon for the next fifteen years of my life. Always questioning another's love, wondering when I would be discarded once they'd had their fill. However, I accepted these terms; I accepted them because the people with whom I came into contact weren't the only ones deriving something from it. Just one act of kindness would wipe away the pain, take away the sorrow, fill my heart with hope and breathe life into my soul. That's all it ever took because, to me, even when I was being raped, at least, for that brief moment, I was also wanted.

Jim's skin glided against mine as he slid between my legs.

"If I hurt you, then tell me," he whispered.

I began to feel really nervous. I desperately wanted to please him, but also, I needed him to want me.

"O.K" I replied.

"Ere, sniff some of this, it'll help you relax," he said holding the bottle under my nose.

I sniffed up hard, nostrils opened wide as the fumes from the Isobutyl Nitrate spewed into my lungs. My heart rate tripled in speed as the drug reached a climax in my body. My face tightened and felt as though it was swelling so much it might explode at any given time.

"Good feeling, eh?" Jim said pressing himself up against me.

My body felt just so very relaxed as he pushed himself inside me but, even with the drug, I found it hard not to tighten my eyes as he pressed further and further inside. He was so gentle, holding me, looking into my eyes the whole time.

"Do you know how to cum?" he asked, as he moved his hips back and forth.

"No," I answered, embarrassed.

"I'll show you," he whispered.

He began to move his hand over me and then, in an up and down motion, he began to masturbate me. It felt so good: a feeling of complete pleasure. After a while, I began to experience an immense feeling of wanting to let go, to give in to the sensations that flooded the lower part of my body, almost a tickling too much to bear. I wanted to let go so badly.

"Relax yourself and then, when the tickling feeling really gets too much to bear, you need to tense yourself and THEN let go," he explained.

"Oh my God, I can't believe this feeling," I said excitedly.

Why had no one else told me about this? I really had been used for their own pleasure hadn't I? They weren't interested in me and how I felt. At least Jim wanted me to enjoy this moment too.

At the moment of climax, Jim gave me another sniff of the 'poppers' and told me to tell him when I was going to cum. The blood rushed to my head as I looked lovingly into Jim's eyes. He was making love to me and it felt amazing. He gripped me tighter as he ground himself harder against me. This feeling became too much to bear.

"I need to let go, I'm going to…. I'm…" I screamed.

Quickly, he put his hand gently over my mouth. Fluids rushed through my penis to the surface like a volcano waiting to explode.

We both climaxed at the exact same time.

Tears began to flood my eyes. I felt so happy; so fulfilled.

That feeling, right there, right then, I would never forget and never want to forget. Wrongly, I would test this moment and feeling in future relationships because, at the end of the day, I was still only a fourteen-year old boy. I didn't care. I wanted this man so much. I never wanted to be without him. He was my hero, the one to whom I would look up from this day forward. He had just made love to me and taught me how to masturbate – and love myself.

"Did you enjoy that?" he whispered in my ear as we lay arm in arm.

"So much," I replied in a mesmerised state.

"I want us to do that every night," he said.

"Really?" I asked.

"Really…. I'm in love with you"

He said it! He actually said it.

He LOVES ME.

For the next two weeks we made love every night. He would go upstairs to do his marital duties with Julie while I waited downstairs, and then, we would get close. The only part of it, which I didn't like, was never being able to wake up beside him. What we were doing was risky enough, but to get caught in the morning cuddled up close was way too much of a risk.

During this two- week affair, Michael had left for London. He seemed quite happy that I was staying with Jim and knew what was going on between us. I saw Jamie only one more time. He turned up from Liverpool after having been away for five days. I could have been dead for all he knew or cared. I was too scared to be anywhere close to him anyway. He came round to say goodbye before he and Michael left, but it felt really strange saying goodbye to them I never saw or heard from either of them again, although my time with Jamie would be brought up in a police matter three years later. Never had I thought that, what had started out as a holiday would end up with me staying there.

Through the day I would sit and watch television with my new family. I met Jim's sister and went to both Jim and Julie's family "get-together" at the weekend. I really felt as though I was with a loving family; and that I had somewhere to belong.

Each night that Jim would see Julie off to bed became increasingly difficult for me. The thought of them lying together made my stomach churn. It was worse on the nights when I could hear the banging of the bed, as the noise rattled down the wall and echoed into the living room below where I was sitting waiting, in tears. The tear in my heart would grow bigger as each bang was heard. How could he do this to me? Why? Didn't he love me anymore?

One night, after listening to them doing 'it' for what seemed like a lifetime, I became angry. Eventually, Jim came into the living room where I was sitting and could see that I was distressed.

"What's wrong?" he said looking at the upset written all over my face.

"Don't you love me anymore?" I asked, tears starting to roll down my face.

"Of course I do!" he assured me, as he walked over to the sofa to comfort me.

"Then why do you have sex with her?" I asked, sobbing.

"You know I have to do it to keep her happy, so that she doesn't suspect anything," he answered.

"I hate it! I wish it was just you and me," I, almost, whimpered.

"One day it will be. I promise," he said.

"What do you mean?" I was taken by surprise.

What did he mean? He was going to leave Julie? Run away with me?

"I've been thinking," he said in a hushed voice.

"What?" I asked in anticipation.

"I've got a little test going on in my head," he answered.

He went on to explain to me that he had come up with this little 'test' that would let him know -and me know- when we could be together. I was such an idiot to believe that this test idea he was telling me about would actually work. He told me that Julie would start with fifteen points and, every time she annoyed him, she would have points taken away. Once she reached zero, he would leave her.

Every night, I would ask how many points she had left until it became an obsession, eating away at my mind, driving me to hate her more and more as the days went past.

The days went by and the evenings became more about the points than taking the time to enjoy his company. Soon, she had only six points left.

"It won't be long now," he said to me, as he kissed me goodnight.

This whole thing was becoming a routine : sit up, get Julie off to bed, listen to them having sex for half an hour, cry, get naked, lie on the floor and 'make love', ask how many points she had left, kiss goodnight and then start the whole process again the following day. Still, I was madly in love with him; it's only when I look back, now, that I can see how I truly felt.

The next night, however, was different. After we had 'made love' I asked the usual "point" question. I was shocked by the reply I received.

"You started with fifteen points as well," he said smiling.

"What?" I answered quickly.

"When I gave her points, I gave you 'em as well," he answered still smiling.

I thought he was joking, but he wasn't. He said that he had to give us both points so that it was fair, and that this would be the only real way to find out whom he wanted to be with for the rest of his life. I couldn't believe it. Why was he testing me? He didn't want me anymore, did he? He was using this as an excuse to get rid of me and to make me feel that I had done it to myself. He was just like the rest, wasn't he? He was trying to break me. But I loved him. I wanted to be with him.

From that night on, I so desperately tried to please him. I did anything he asked me to do because I was so scared that I would lose more points than her. I made an extra effort to be nice to Julie herself because, in my head, I was going to succeed in taking Jim anyway. I wouldn't mess up.

At least I thought I wouldn't.

But I did……big-time!

One night, we were going to meet Julie's brother and his family - I don't remember any of their names. When we arrived, I was introduced to her brother and his wife and their two daughters, who were slightly younger than me. While the 'adults' were talking, I went upstairs with the two girls. The conversation is very vague in my mind and not really that important to this story. We must have been up there for over an hour when Julie shouted up the stairs to let me know that it was time to go; as I stood up to leave, one of the girls passed me a small crucifix.

"I want you to have this 'cos I like ya," she said in a now very familiar Liverpool accent.

"Thanks," I said as I took the gift.

"Don't tell mi ma like. She'll kill us for giving it away," she said smiling.

"I won't. I'll hide it in my pocket" I replied.

I made my way down the stairs and said goodbye to everyone and then left with Jim, Julie and the kids.

"Where am I going to hide the bloody thing? It's not like I have my own cupboards, is it!"

Once we'd arrived back at the house, I went straight into the living room and quickly hid the crucifix under the sofa. I don't really know to this day why I accepted it. What was I going to do with it?

Just at that moment, the phone rang. It was Julie's brother. One of the girls had told their mum that their sister had given me her crucifix.

Julie looked at me suspiciously as she placed the phone back on to the receiver.

"Leon?" She was looking right at me.

My heart was racing. I knew exactly what she was going to ask. Why had I allowed myself to be put into this situation? I was so angry with myself. I felt like a thief and yet I hadn't even done anything wrong; but, instead of helping the situation, I made it a thousand times worse by lying. Why did I lie? To be honest, I was simply scared. I thought that even by telling the truth I would just end up looking like a little thief and a liar. Negative feelings started flooding my head. I could hear Jim and Enid's voices echoing round and round, reminding me that I was scum, a no-hoper, a useless twat, stupid, a bastard, a thief, a waste of life and a piece of shit.

"STOP!!!!" I screamed to my 'other' me.

I knew I had to hold it together quickly, as I felt myself slipping into that huge dark hole. I had to lie. I was innocent of any crime, but I had to lie; it was the only way.

"Yeah?" I answered.

"When we were at my brother's, did little Sammy give you something?"

"No," I replied.

"Are you sure about that?" she questioned in an accusing voice.

"Yes," I lied again.

I could tell that she didn't believe me.

All at once, I felt this family situation start to crumble around me. My own guilt was destroying all that was good. I knew that the lying would eat away at my sanity, as it does even to this day. My own conscience kills me and sends me to that dark place in my mind, haunting me with the voices of those who have tried to destroy me, constantly reminding me that I am worthless, and that if I don't do the right thing, then they will have won.

I sat on the back doorstep, in the kitchen, smoking a cigarette, while Jim and Julie went through into the living room.

I began to cry.

Why did she give me the stupid thing anyway and WHY did I take it? I had known, deep down, that it would be trouble because they had made me hide it. Now, if I owned up, it would make me look even more guilty.

What if it was a set up? What if Julie had figured out that I was having sex with her husband and she had told the girls to give me the cross and then get me into trouble by saying I'd stolen it?

Or, maybe the girls hadn't liked me and they had set me up for a joke?

Maybe it was Jim who had set the whole thing up to make sure that I lost all of my points so that he could tell me to go?

"STOP!!!" I screamed to my 'other' me inside my head.

I'm going to destroy myself and destroy this situation, if I keep this locked in any longer. I had to act.

"Jim!" I shouted from the kitchen into the living room, loud enough to be heard, but not enough to wake the kids.

Jim appeared at the kitchen door and leaned against it.

"What is it?" he asked.

"I've got something to tell you," I said with my eyes glaring into the floor, too embarrassed to look up.

"You nicked that crucifix didn't you?" he said directly.

"NO…I didn't steal it. She gave me it…. Honest" I stuttered.

"Honest…if you were honest then you wouldn't have lied in the first place," he answered in a disappointed manner.

He was right. How did it look from his point of view? If only I had told them the truth.

Why did I screw everything up all of the time?

I'm pathetic.

I'm weak.

A lost cause.

I'd done it now. I'd shown them I was a dirty liar. I felt so embarrassed that I'd opened up the real me: the real person whom only Jim and Enid had truly recognised.

"I'm so sorry," I gulped, in my pathetic little voice.

Jim looked at me in disgust and walked away without saying a word.

What was going to happen now?

" I'm going to be going back to Kirkby Willows aren't I? Where else is there to go? I can't go in a children's home, I'll definitely end up dead, then. Think, think, THINK!"

My thoughts were interrupted when Julie appeared around the door as I was sitting on the doorstep, sobbing.

"I'm so sorry for lying, Julie," I whimpered, as the tears rolled down my face.

"Where is it?" she snapped.

"I hid it under the sofa when we got back in," I answered.

She disappeared into the living room and, a few moments later, Jim reappeared.

"I can't believe you've done this, Leon. How could you steal from a kid?" he said in disgust.

"But I never stole it. She gave me it," I protested.

I could hear Julie on the phone in the background telling whoever it was that she had the crucifix and that I had admitted to taking it.

She reappeared and stood next to Jim, as they both stared at me.

"That was my brother on the phone. I've told him that you've admitted taking it," she said.

"They gave me it…. Honestly," I said.

"Why should we believe you when you lied in the first place?" she asked.

"Because I'm telling the truth. They told me not to tell anyone otherwise, they would get into trouble for giving it away," I answered.

"Do you know why it's such a big deal, Leon?" asked Julie.

I looked blankly at her, awaiting the answer.

"Sammy was given this cross on her death bed," she said.

"She was dying with Leukaemia two years ago," Jim added.

"Cancer…and that cross was given to her by a nun," Julie snapped.

I burst into tears. Why was this happening?

Just then the phone rang. It was Julie's brother again.

"That was my brother on the phone. Lucky for you Sammy has admitted that she gave you the cross. But that doesn't alter the fact that you hid it and lied," she said.

"I'm sorry," I spluttered out between tears.

"I'm going to bed. I've heard enough," she answered.

A few moments after Julie left, Jim turned to me.

"You've got no points left, mate," he said coldly.

He turned and followed after Julie. He never came back down that night. I was alone.

"How could he be so fucking cruel?" I hissed to myself.

Anger started to eat away at me. I fell asleep that night in tears and a mind heavy with fear. Where would I go from here? How would I survive? Why should he get away with doing this to me! He had said that he loved me and that we were going to live together.

I felt so lost that night, so confused and so angry. Why didn't I just say I'd been given the damn crucifix in the first place.

Blackout.

I opened my eyes and saw Julie sitting on the armchair opposite me, smoking a cigarette.

"Morning," she said.

"Morning," I answered.

"Jim and me have been talking," she started.

Where was Jim?

"Where's Jim?" I interrupted.

"He's had to go out.... We've decided...you're gonna have to go," she said coldly.

"WHAT!" I screamed.

Fear gripped my heart so hard that I thought I was going to pass out. It was like a large fist clenching my insides. My head started to throb as I took in the words that were coming from her mouth.

"Go where?" I added as the tears began to flow.

"I don't know…. But you can't stay here," she added.

"WHERE'S Jim?" I screamed. He would put a stop to this. He wouldn't let her throw me out. Or would he?

"I've told you -Jim had to go out. He thought it was better if he wasn't here when I told you," she replied.

I couldn't believe it! I wanted him to appear and tell me it was all going to be o.k.

He didn't.

Julie had packed all my belongings while I had still been asleep. This was it. I was being thrown out and I had nowhere to go. I was scared and wanted to lash out. Julie told me to go and get ready.

The next thirty minutes went into a blur as I got ready and gathered my things together. I was shaking uncontrollably.

"Here's some money to get you on your way," she said, passing me two five pound notes.

Tears rolled down my face as I left the house that had become my home.

I was never to see Jim or his family again after that day.

I walked down the street in a state of shock. How could everything go so wrong, so quickly? I'd done this. It was my entire fault. AGAIN.

I hated myself. I wandered aimlessly through the streets of Magna, not knowing which way to turn or what to do. My heart felt as though it was breaking into a thousand pieces, like the shards of glass from a bottle when it hits the stone floor.

I was broken, from the inside out.

People, everywhere I look. I feel trapped, finding it hard to breathe, my lungs folding inward like a balloon having the air suctioned from it. Who are all these people? Where are they going? Who are they going to see? Are they happy? Are they sad? Do they have nice homes to go to? Are they lonely?

I am.

I am so lonely. All I see right now is darkness, a darkness closing in on me, stealing my life from me, taking it without any warning. The rain has started: it's running down my face like an uncontrollable river. The swishing sound from the car wheels racing through the puddles on the road gets louder in my mind.

I'm so cold.

My skin is turning purple and red, like the colour of corned beef. My arms sting as I rub them to warm them up and get the blood circulating.

Is this it? Is this what I ran away for? Going back to Kirkby Willows didn't sound so bad now.

What do I do?

Before I know it, I am walking into a large building: it's the Magna Police headquarters. What's the worst that can happen? I go to prison for running away? Big deal, I've already survived one prison. I walk aimlessly into the main reception area. Wherever I look there are people. Why can't they all piss off and mind their own business? Leave me alone to rot. It's what I was put on this planet for, isn't it?

Just then my thoughts of self- pity are interrupted.

"Can I help?" enquired a deep voice.

I looked up and was face to face with a policeman. Without even thinking my mouth did the work for me.

"I've run away from home and I think the police are looking for me," I said in a lifeless and numb voice.

"You want Social Services, lad," he replied. "Great!" I thought to myself." Even the fucking police aren't interested. I bet I haven't even been reported missing. What use is there in this thing called life? Why am I actually here?"

Before I even had time to answer my own questions, I looked up to a blank space in front of me. The policeman had already walked away to take another enquiry.

"Wanker!" I muttered, under my breath, as I walked back out of the building.

So now where?

It's getting dark now and I'm beginning to feel frightened. Miscellaneous questions start to swirl round in my head: why did my dad really kill himself? Why was I not given the chance to have him and my mum to look after me?

I'm angry, hurt, upset, lonely, tired and hungry. I just want to be loved.

I wander around the streets and realise the time. It's five 'o' clock and the offices are going to be closing soon. What if I don't find it in time? I am so tired and drained. Only two days ago I was in the arms of Jim, in the warm, safe from harm. Now, due to telling lies, I am on the streets in the dark. I've lost everything.

My self-loathing is at an all-time high. I hate myself. I hate being me. I have visions of slicing my own face off with a blunt knife, carving away at my rotting flesh, ripping my hair out, clump after clump, slashing my skin with rusty razor, punching at my own arms and legs, gorging my eyes out with my own fingers and then, afterwards, getting some pliers and tearing out my fingernails. As I read that, now, it seems melodramatic but, at that time, I just wanted to squeeze every vestige of life from my filthy heart. I remember thinking: Lord, please let me just die. I don't want to be here anymore, I'm through with it all. I've had enough of the pain, the hurt, the loneliness, the fear of being hurt and abused: the pain of a fully- grown man fucking the life out of me. Fucking me so hard I bleed inside. No-one can see the pain from the outside. It's all inside me. In me, in my thoughts: thoughts which will torture me until eternity. I don't want to feel the pain anymore. I want to be left alone. What pleasure does someone get when they hurt another human being?

A child!

Me!

After beating my own head with venomous thoughts, my survival instincts kick back in.

"Show them…. Show them all…. They won't beat me…. I won't give them the satisfaction…. It's me against them…. Play them like they play you," I say to my 'other' me through gritted teeth.

My hurt has turned to anger now. I will survive this for one reason and one reason only: to beat them.

They want to destroy me. They want me to give in.

I won't do it.

I won't be beaten.

EVER.

After asking lots of people for directions, finally, I find the Social Services building. It's after quarter past five now. I still have time. I stand outside for a few minutes to gather my thoughts and wipe away my caked-on tears.

What do I say?

Where have I been?

I decide, at this point, that I won't tell them anything other than that I've been sleeping rough. I had already been told by Jim, after the first time we had done 'it', that if I told anyone about what we were doing, his family would be furious, find me wherever I went, track me down and cut my throat. He said that I needn't worry though, because he knew that I loved him and that I would never do something like that. At the time when he said it, I didn't even feel like I was been threatened.

I walked in to find a woman behind the reception desk. No sooner had she said, "Can I help?" than I burst into tears. She rushed around the desk to comfort me. Only at this point did I realise how drained I truly felt. This was it: I'd done it; I'd handed myself in. I didn't really care what happened now. I just wanted to be safe and warm.

After making me a cup of tea, the on-duty social worker phoned my new social worker, who I didn't really know, as she had just taken the post shortly before I ran away. It was arranged that that she would come and pick me up the next day and take it from there.

"She will pick you up tomorrow, Leon" said the social worker.

"What do I do tonight? I've got nowhere to stay?" I asked.

"Don't worry, love, there's a small residential home not far from here.

You can rest your head there tonight," she said in a reassuring tone.

"Residential?" I said with a look of confusion on my face.

"It's just a bit like a big family," she added smiling.

I gave her a half-smile back.

After a few minutes, we left for the home. The longer we drove the more familiar the streets became. This was the way to Jim's house. Why were we coming this way? Was it a trap? Did she know Jim?

I became frightened.

"Where are you taking me?" I demanded.

"To the home. It's just up here," she said pulling into the pavement.

The home was literally a stone's throw away from Jim's house.

Without warning, my lungs seemed to collapse as I tried to draw breath.

The harder I tried to fight for breath, the more of a struggle it became. It suddenly dawned on me that Jim might think I'd told them about what he and I had been up to, and I hadn't. I hadn't breathed a word.

"I can't stay here!" I screamed.

"Leon! What's wrong?" she asked.

"He'll think I've told you everything! They will come and get me! Please let me go somewhere else. PLEASE!" I shouted.

"Leon, Leon please calm down, no-one is going to hurt you here. You will be safe", she said in an attempt to calm me down.

I slumped into the car seat like a sack of abandoned belongings.

"Is that the place where you stayed, Leon? Around that corner?" she probed.

"Yeah…But they looked after me…they were kind to me," I said in their

defence.

"Then why are you so frightened?" she asked in a gentle voice.

"Because…. Because we fell out and I had to leave…I just want to tell them I'm sorry…They didn't know I'd run away" I explained.

"Where DID they think you had come from then?" she asked.

I shrugged my shoulders. She knew I was lying, but she couldn't do much about it because, unless I told her everything, then nothing could be done to them. I told her that they thought I was just a homeless lad who had fallen out with his parents and ended up on the streets.

"That was very kind of them then," she said.

"They were kind," I replied.

"Do you want to say goodbye to them?" she asked.

My heart sank. I knew that, when I had left earlier that day, even if I did want to see them, they wouldn't want to see me; not after all the trouble

I'd caused to them. Why would they?

"No…. It's ok…I better just leave them now," I said as tears began to roll down my face.

"If you're sure?" she replied.

"Yeah…. I'm sure," I said.

She leaned over and wiped the tear from my face.

"Come on then," she said, clapping her hands and smiling to lighten the mood.

We stepped out of the car and walked up the long, winding path to the front door of the home. A tall woman answered the door. She let us in and then showed me around the house, introducing me to the five other kids who were staying there. I couldn't quite believe what I was seeing. This was no backdrop for the setting of "Oliver Twist". This was the most normal 'home' I'd ever come across. Yet again, another one of Jim and Enid's lies had made me believe the worst.

After settling me in to my home for the night, the social worker left. I never did catch her name but, if she is reading this book and the story sounds familiar, then I want to say, "Thank you for your kind-heartedness on that day".

That night, I spent most of my time watching T.V. and chatting to the other kids. Most of them had never had parents and the ones who did had major problems with them. All of a sudden, I didn't feel so alone. I wasn't a complete weirdo for being fostered.

I wished I could see Beverly now, show her this home and let her see what I was seeing. If she had seen that, then she wouldn't have had to go through another four years of abuse: horrific abuse. It took her fifteen years to tell me – finally - what had gone on in that house.

I missed her that night.

As I lay in these unfamiliar surroundings, I felt a sense of relief for giving myself up. Not having to run again made me a little more relaxed and, that feeling, gave me the chance to use my energy trying to mend my broken heart. If only I had known then that it would take over another decade, I would have been more prepared.

I fell into a deep sleep.

The next day came around so quickly. The sun was shining through a tear in the curtain and onto my face.

"Where am I?" I asked my 'other' me.

"It's o.k. We've survived," I answered.

And we had. Me and my 'other' me were both alive.

"I wonder what is going to happen, today?" I thought.

"Will I be going back to Kirkby Willows?"

It's quite strange, because I still remember, vividly, that the feeling of fear towards Jim and Enid seemed less powerful when I woke up that day. Nothing felt as bad as it had done the day before and I didn't feel scared to go back to Kirkby Willows. It's almost as though, when I had gone to bed that night, all of my fears disappeared too.

I felt quite good when I woke up. In fact I was quite taken aback by how

'O.K.' I actually felt.

What I didn't realise at the time was that my mind wanted - and needed - familiar surroundings and faces for me truly to let go; this was merely my mind protecting me from the events that had happened over the previous couple of weeks. My mind and my body were still in shock from the multiple rapes I had endured. If only I had held on to that feeling of peace in my mind. The feeling that no matter how bad someone tries to make you feel, you can hold your head up and smile, because peace of mind is a tool more powerful than anything on this earth.

I was fourteen years old and I was on the verge of a nervous breakdown.

This was merely the calm before the storm.

Blackout.

"Penny!" I shrieked as one of the home carers brought my social worker through the front door. I ran over to her and hugged her so tightly I almost squeezed the life out of her. I didn't even know her that well, yet it felt so comfortable to be in her arms.

"Oh, Leon!" she said, holding me just as tightly.

I cried for what seemed like an eternity; non-stop, flowing tears.

"Are you o.k?" she added as tears welled up in her eyes.

She actually cared that I was ok and was genuinely pleased to see me.

That made me feel really special, a woman who barely knew me was becoming emotional after seeing I was o.k.

"I'm SO happy to see you, Penny," I whimpered.

We sat down for a while and I told her all about my time away, but missed out some of the more ugly details. After a cup of coffee, we gathered my few belongings and headed out to her car.

"Where are we going?" I asked.

"That's up to you, Leon" she replied.

"What do you mean?" I asked.

"Well, there are two choices; and it really is YOUR choice as to where we go. You can go back to Kirkby Willows or there is a home in Canton, called Croft House, where there is room for you until a place in a family unit home becomes available," she replied. "Croft House?" I asked.

She went on to explain that, until a place came up in the family unit home, I would be placed in Croft House which was a young offenders' institute.

"I don't want to go to prison!" I yelled.

"It's not a prison, it's just a not as nice as the other places," she explained.

Some choice! I can go back to Kirkby Willows or a young offenders' institute.

I decided.

"I'll go back to Kirkby Willows," I said.

Even as the words poured out of my mouth, I couldn't actually believe that I was saying them.

After everything that bastard had done to me, I now wanted to go back!

Why?

I decided there and then that, perhaps, things would be different; that they would be o.k. with me when I returned. I also took into account that I was a different person now and that, even if things weren't different, I would just run away again. After everything I had endured over the last few weeks I knew I was capable of leaving again and that, if I had to, it would be for the last time. I missed my sister and I wanted to see her. I was in for a surprise!

"You're sure?" she asked.

"Yeah, I'm sure" I replied.

In the car, Penny and I chatted and I told her all about Jim and Julie and that I was going to miss them so much.

"Why do you think you will miss them?" she asked.

"They were so good to me…I'd never felt like part of a family until I stayed with them," I answered.

It was true. I had never felt like part of a family until that time with them.

I longed for Jim to hold me close and tell me everything was going to be o.k. Everything had changed in such a short space of time.

As we drew nearer to Kirkby Willows, the inside of my stomach, increasingly, felt like a washing machine doing a full spin cycle. I was so nervous about seeing them again. Strangely, however, I wasn't feeling scared; just nervous. I had been on the run for almost six weeks. So much had happened in that time: my whole life had been turned upside down and shaken about. I didn't realise how much I, as a person, had changed too.

We pulled up outside the only-too-familiar, blue-glossed front door.

"I'm so nervous," I said to Penny as we crossed the main road over to the house.

"It's going to be o.k. Leon," she said, giving me a warm smile.

I didn't know what to do.

Do I just walk in?

Do I knock?

I wasn't sure that walking in was a good idea as I really didn't feel as though I belonged there anymore. I decided to knock.

The door swung open.

"Hello, stranger," said the familiar face.

It was Enid. I didn't have a clue what to say to her! However, one thing that did take me by surprise was the way I felt inside at that very moment.

I felt nothing. No emotion seemed to sweep across my mind. No fear, no remorse, no guilt and, definitely, no love.

"Hiya!" I blurted out.

"Come in then," she said, holding the door open.

"Ta!" I walked through the door and into the living room.

"Nothing has changed here," I thought to myself, as Enid and Penny chatted in the hallway. I just sat there staring at the cheap, brass-effect, ornamental horses that were sitting on the mantelpiece, which had been their home for as long as I could remember.

After about half an hour, Penny popped her head around the corner to say goodbye.

"I'll come and see you next week, Leon…. It's so good to see you," she said as she left.

"Thanks Penny…. See you next week," I replied.

I then heard the front door close.

"Do you want a coffee?" Enid asked, as she peered through the living room door.

"No thanks," I answered.

She came and sat down in the armchair opposite the sofa where I was sitting.

"So, what did you get up to on your little holiday?" she asked in a sarcastic tone.

I just shrugged my shoulders, as I really couldn't be bothered making idle chit-chat; and why should I anyway? We were always made to sit in silence between the hours of six pm and nine pm while they watched their programmes, and now, here she was sitting and wanting to chat. No chance! I said very little for the next hour other than to answer 'yes', 'no' or 'I don't know'.

…….until I heard the front door close. .

It's him!

'Stay calm…he can't hurt you,' I told my 'other' me.

The living room door creaked slowly as it opened.

I was right.

It was him.

"Hello stranger," he said with that sickly smirk on his face.

I really did hate him. I felt sick looking at him. How could he just stand there and act like nothing had happened? Pretending we were the best of friends.

What a bastard!

"Hiya!" I said through gritted teeth.

He came further into the living room and sat down.

"Enjoy your holiday?" he asked, still smirking.

I gave a half-hearted smile.

It certainly didn't take Enid long to drop the pleasantries.

"What you being so bloody quiet for?" she snapped.

"I'm tired," I replied.

"Leave him be. He's just back," Jim added.

Had I just witnessed him sticking up for me? What was his game this time? Maybe he was genuinely fighting my corner.

Not likely. Anyway, I wouldn't be sticking around long enough to bother. The answer soon became clear.

"Aren't you going to ask where your sister is?" he prodded, with a look of pure evil in his face.

Before I had even answered, Enid butted in.

"She's escaped from the sight of you!" she sneered.

"What?" I asked in a cocky tone.

"She got in to Art College in Canton. She moved there two weeks ago," he announced.

I looked puzzled.

"That's right. She's gone," Enid added.

"And do you know what? Your own sister left here hating YOU!" he said with pure venom.

'It's not true. They are lying,' I said over and over again in my head to my 'other' me.

"I'm going to bed," I announced, as I stood up.

That was the first time in that house that I had SAID I was doing something, rather than asking permission first. They didn't say a word. They just looked at me like I was a piece of shit. Nothing changed there then. Suddenly, something dawned on me.

I felt no fear! That was it! That was the strange feeling I had. For the first time in my life, within these walls that had been my prison and my nightmare for fourteen years, I had NO FEAR!

Fear or no fear, that night, I cried myself to sleep.

So did my only true blood family member really leave hating me? I'd only been back a day and already their poisonous words were destroying me. I wouldn't let them see it, though. No way would they ever see that they were getting to me.

The next morning I opened my eyes and my whole body shot upright. I'd forgotten that I was back there, for a split second, and panicked when I saw the familiar surroundings. I closed my eyes tightly in the hope that, when I opened them; I would really be back at Jim and Julie's house and that this would be just a horrible nightmare.

It didn't work.

When I opened my eyes, I was still in the shit hole they called a home. I dressed and made my way down the stairs and into the kitchen. I saw Enid in the front living room, through the crack in the door, but didn't bother to acknowledge the fact that I'd seen her. What was the point? I had nothing to say to her anyway.

I poured myself some cereal into a bowl and began to eat.

Bang.

The inside of my heart tore open without warning.

I want Jim.

I need him.

I'm never going to see him again, am I?

"WHY?" I screamed out loud, unable to control my emotions.

I began to smash my head on the kitchen table. Over and over again, I head-butted the table. I was losing all sense of reality. Enid came running through the kitchen door.

"What the hell do you think you're doing?" she shrieked.

"I FUCKING HATE YOU!" I screamed back at her.

"I fucking hate you and your BASTARD husband and your house and everything in it! I HATE YOU!!!!!!" I screamed over and over.

She moved away sharply, as I rose from the chair. I wanted to hit her so hard, repeatedly, over and over, I wanted to smash her face into a thousand tiny pieces.

"LEON! Calm down!" she screamed back with a look of pure terror in her face.

"I hate you!" I screamed right in her face as she cowered into the corner of the kitchen wall.

I fell to the floor, shaking with anger. Holding my head in my hands, I curled up into a tight ball, rocking backwards and forwards. My head felt as though it was going to explode. What was happening to me? Was I finally losing my mind? Was this all life had to offer? Torment? A living hell?

These were my first steps into what would become a deep depression.

Enid stood upright.

"What happened to you when you were away?" she asked as the terror lifted from her face.

"I miss Jim and Julie," I whimpered.

"GREAT!" she yelled at me.

Great? What did she mean by great?

"After everything we've done for you and you miss some strangers who you've only known for five minutes" she whined.

I had absolutely nothing else to say.

Inside I had already died. My soul was tired: worn out beyond repair.

I'm never going to see them again, am I? What was has now been and gone, never to return. I had been loved; and I threw it all away with one stupid lie. I spent the next few days in a kind of mourning for what I had just lost.

I was due to return to my old school for a meeting with the head-mistress, Mrs. Franton. Walking into that school for the first time since being away was hard. I felt like my world had collapsed. Everything that had happened seemed to have been like watching the end of a movie. I was back - and everything and everyone was exactly the same.

Everyone, that was, except me.

I had to do something to end this torment. I couldn't come back to this school; not now after everything I had been through. I couldn't bear the thought of all those faces staring at me with those accusing-looks and all of the questions that would follow.

I had to escape this hell.

I had to do something to change this chain of events. I didn't belong here anymore. I didn't belong anywhere in this world. Where would I find my true self?

I made a decision, there and then - while I was in the office, staring out of the window, looking at the large, monkey-puzzle tree in the school garden. Looking, through tired, swollen, red eyes, puffy from the non-stop tears I had shed for days, if not weeks; I had no choice but to run again. I didn't even know where to run or to what, but I knew I had to go.

And I did.

After returning to the house and having some tea, I made my way up to my bedroom. As I was walking towards my door, I noticed that Jim and Enid's bedroom door wasn't locked. They had started locking it for the last couple of years because they said that "nothing was sacred in this house because of the two little thieving bastards who lived here," - those two being Beverly and me.

I took my opportunity while it was there. I sneaked into their room, on tiptoes and, no sooner had I gone in, than I heard the living room open, followed by footsteps climbing the stairs.

"Shit!" I hissed at my 'other' me. I was going to get caught in the act if whoever it was coming up those stairs didn't go to the toilet first.

I stood there, behind the door, frozen with the fear of being caught. Whoever it was coming up the stairs wasn't stopping off for the toilet. I rushed across their bedroom floor and hid behind the bed. The bedroom door opened. I couldn't see who it was for the fear of being seen trying to take a look.

My heart was racing faster than the wheels of a car in a grand prix. I was sure that I would be caught as the pounding of my heart grew louder and louder. Suddenly, the door closed and the click of the lock echoed into the room.

"Shit!" I cursed as the penny dropped in my mind.

I hadn't been caught, but what had happened was far worse.

I was now locked inside the bedroom with no key to get back out.

I had to think quickly. Panicking, I rummaged through their drawers, in search of anything that would help me to escape from this place. I succeeded in finding £7.00 in one of the drawers and a packet of Benson and Hedges cigarettes.

This was it.

This was my final goodbye to Kirkby Willows.

Slowly, I opened their bedroom window, trying so hard not to make a single noise. I was going to have to climb across part of the lower roof and over the wall at the bottom of the yard. Thank God it was dark, because, if it had been light, then the living-room windows would have been open and I would have been caught for sure.

For the second time, I'd broken my promise to God.

I ran in the opposite direction to the one which I'd run when I ended up in

London. I didn't even have a plan and, to be honest, I didn't care. I slowed my pace as I drew closer to Kirkby Willows town centre. There wasn't much there: two newsagents, a furniture shop and a few trinket shops. There was also a large church in the centre, with a pathway leading to the other side of town. On this pathway were some public toilets - three in total - one for the ladies, one for the gents and a larger one for the disabled. I made my way over to the disabled one. I knew that I wouldn't be bothered there as it was a single unit. As I crept inside, I could smell cheap bleach. The stench stuck in my throat, clinging onto it like a leech does to fresh flesh. This would be my home for the night. I would figure out what to do in the morning.

I rolled up my jumper, made it into a pillow, then lay down on the ice-cold tiles, huddling myself up tightly, making sure to keep as much body heat as possible. Having been locked in their bedroom, I hadn't had the luxury of grabbing my jacket and other warm items of clothing.

"It's so cold," I whispered to my 'other' me.

What was I doing with my life? Why could I not just be happy? I remember lying there, shivering, wishing I could turn life's clock back to the time before my real dad committed suicide and that God would stop him from doing it, so that all of this wouldn't be real and I'd be at home with my proper family.

People always say that things happen for a reason or that God tests us with different scenarios to see how we cope. I wished that he wouldn't test me anymore. Hadn't I had enough of that in London and Liverpool? Maybe I was just one of those losers to whom everything happened because I was simply 'bad stock' and deserved no more than this.

"Where will I actually go tomorrow?

It doesn't matter. Not now. I've decided to take whatever comes my way".

That night I drifted in and out of a light sleep. I would blow into my hands and rub them together to stop them from going numb. At times I cried and, in sheer desperation and temper, I would start to punch the tiled walls of the toilet.

"There must be something out there that will bring me happiness?"

Blackout.

"You don't deserve any happiness. You're BAD STOCK!" Jim screamed.

"LEAVE ME ALONE!!!!"

I wake up screaming uncontrollably, shaking with fear. It had just been a nightmare.

I wake up from one nightmare into another.

I'm lying shivering on the toilet floor.

It's morning now.

I tried to get up, but my legs stayed still. At first, I panicked because I thought they'd frozen to the floor tiles.

"It's just pins and needles," I said out loud as I rubbed them.

It was so cold that night that it took me seven or eight minutes to be able to function properly and, even after that time, I still couldn't feel my nose and ears. I unlatched the lock on the toilet door and swung the door open.

"Where are you off to this time?" asked the policeman standing in my pathway.

"Shit!" I cursed, as I realised there was no escape.

"That's enough of the swearing," he growled.

"Sorry!" I said, as defeat crept into my mind.

I couldn't believe it! I must be losing my touch. Last time I was away for almost five to six weeks and this time I hadn't even lasted twenty-four hours. When I look back at that night, in the toilets, I almost knew at the time that I wasn't going to be on the run for long. Something told me that, subconsciously. Of course, I was still surprised when I opened the door to a policeman. I didn't see that one coming!

After being taken to the station, a cup of tea was made for me. The warmth from the room heaters made my skin sting, as I felt every millimetre of my body come back to life. The tea from the cup felt as though it was melting into my skin.

"Your parents are on their way," said the policeman.

I just rolled my eyes. I didn't even have the energy to care just now. They could say or do what they liked to me; it was of little importance in the larger scheme of things. I didn't even know what I'd be doing tomorrow; to get to the end of today felt like a huge burden enough.

After about half an hour, Jim and Enid arrived.

"Come on, you," Jim said in an unusually up-tempo manner.

What was he looking so pleased about this time? What was in store for me now?

I rose from the chair and made my way to the car which was parked outside. As we drove out of the station, we turned left instead of right.

"Where are we going?" I asked.

"We are going to Pendal to see Penny," snarled Enid.

"What for?" I asked.

"You'll see," smirked Jim.

What were they up to?

I was about to receive the shock of my life.

Blackout.

It took around an hour to reach the Social Services head office in Pendal. The car journey was done in complete silence. I could see Jim's evil eyes through the interior mirror of the car. I don't think it is possible to hate anyone as much as I hated him. The emotion of hate eats away at you from the inside out. It is such a destructive emotion to possess.

When we arrived at the office we were greeted by a man called Nigel who took Jim and Enid into one room, while I had to go upstairs and wait in the other office. Penny was waiting for me up there. I still had the stench of bleach, both on my clothes and up my nose, from sleeping rough in the toilets.

"Hello, you," she said as we walked through the door. She held her arms out to give me a hug.

"Hiya!" I said, forcing a smile. I was really tired and just wanted the luxury of falling asleep in a warm, comfortable bed.

"This is Amy," she said, as she pointed to a woman behind one of the office desks.

"She's going to give you some biscuits, and a nice cup of hot chocolate, while I nip down to speak to Jim and Enid. O.K?" she added.

"O.K." I replied.

I sat in the room doing normal kids activities such as colouring in a picture and completing dot-to-dot puzzles. They had always been my favourite. After about forty minutes, Penny returned with an awkward look on her face.

"Leon?" she said.

"Yes" I answered.

"Come and sit down, love," she said.

I sat down at the table, as Nigel walked in. The three of us sat together.

"I need to explain something to you," said Nigel.

"What is it?" I asked.

"Well, things haven't been going well for you of late, have they? You've had a lot of problems and haven't been happy for a long time, have you?"

These were statements rather than questions.

"No… No I haven't," I answered.

"Which is why these issues need to be resolved," Penny added.

"The thing is…." Nigel started, but was interrupted.

"The thing is…Jim and Enid have gone back home now," she said, gently.

"What do you mean?" I asked, even though, in my mind, I already knew the answer, but needed to hear it for myself.

"You're going to be placed in residential care," she answered.

"Where?" I asked, as tears welled up in my eyes.

"Croft House."

"WHAT!" I screamed.

"It's only short term, Leon. Please don't worry," she answered.

"But I'll get killed in there! I It's a prison. You told me it was!" I said with sheer terror in my voice.

My whole body began to shake and my head began to pound with the pressure of everything that I was taking in. I didn't want to be with those bastards, but I didn't want to go to a young person's prison either. Fourteen years they had been my 'Mum' and 'Dad' and they had known why they were bringing me to this office. They knew and had said nothing. They didn't even say goodbye to me. Isn't that the least they could have done? They had already caused me irreparable damage; then, just like that, after fourteen years, they had brought me here and hadn't even" had the balls" to tell me themselves that they were handing me back to the place from where I had come. I was an orphan when they took me, a six-month old baby dependent on love and nurturing. Now, thirteen- and- a- half-years later I was handed back, still an orphan but even worse now; I was "damaged goods".

I couldn't take all this in, it was too much to bear. I was left with nothing, nothing other than a bag full of issues and memories of abuse.

"WHY...? WHY...? Wwww?" I pleaded over and over as I grabbed onto Penny's arm for answers.

She held me so closely that day. Cradling me like a baby in its mother's arms, not letting go for one moment.

The conversation that followed went in one ear and out of the other, as my mind had been numbed with countless emotional blows. Never in my life had I felt so many uncertainties. Even while on the run, in the back of my head I had Kirkby Willows where I could return if it all became too much to bear. Now, I didn't even have that as an "at worst" option. I sat staring out of the window of Penny's car, as she drove me to Canton.

"Come on, pet. Cheer up," she said rubbing my knee.

I started to cry uncontrollably and Penny reacted by pulling the car over to the side of the road.

"Believe in yourself, Leon…You are so much stronger than you think!" she said looking at me.

"I don't feel strong…. I feel useless," I said, snivelling.

"Look at me…Look at me," she said, as she turned my face towards hers.

"You ARE NOT useless…. YOU are SPECIAL," she added.

What was going to become of me?

Who was Leon?

"It's going to be fine," I whispered to my 'other' me.

It was going to be fine.

Wasn't it?

The chippings on the long driveway made a crunching sound as the car wheels slowly drove over them. In front of us was a large, old building the size of a castle. Chimneys all different sizes were spread all over the roof. It looked like a prison or one of those old laundry warehouses.

"It looks horrible!" I said as the panic inside of me grew by the second.

"It's not forever," answered Penny. It was obvious that she was just trying to comfort me.

We stepped out of the car and she passed me a small, brown suitcase.

"What's that for?" I asked.

"Jim and Enid brought it to the office for you," she said.

That was it? Fourteen years of my life in one small, brown suitcase.

I took it from her and started to cry again. I felt so alone. We walked inside and made our way to the office door where we were greeted by a guy called David. He was to be my support worker: if I had any questions or worries I would go to him.

David showed me around the building, which was to be my new home for the meantime. A long dark corridor was ahead of us, which seemed to go on for miles as we strolled down it. On the left, was a room with a pool table. There were about four rough-looking, older lads playing pool and, when we walked in, David introduced me to them. It was obvious that they had little interest in meeting me, as all they did was grunt and nod.

The next room, which was at the end of the corridor, looked so dark and miserable. This was the television room. Inside, there was a large television and approximately fifteen chairs. It looked like a doctor's waiting room. There were no pictures on the walls. Just bare walls covered in wood chip paper and painted in custard - coloured yellow.

Next, we went to the room on the right which took us down another long corridor. David explained to me that this was the school area.

"School?" I asked.

"Yeah. You will be attending this one until you settle in," he answered.

This really did feel like a prison.

Once I'd taken a look at the school, the laundry room, the three kitchens, the shower block and all of the offices, it was time to see my bedroom.

The upstairs was split into two dormitories: one side for the girls and the other for the boys. There were separate bedrooms for the male and female sleep-over-staff.

Thankfully, I was put into a room on my own. It had three other beds in it, but, as the home wasn't full, I had the luxury of having it all to myself.

After seeing most of the building, Penny left me to unpack my belongings.

"I'll come and see you next week, Leon. Try to settle in as best you can," she said, hugging me.

"See you later," I said, as tears welled up in my eyes again.

That was that. Here I was in my new 'home' with my new bedroom and my little brown suitcase. I opened the case to find a few pairs of socks, some underwear, one pair of jeans and three tee shirts. Before I even knew it, I was on the floor, leaning against the bed, sobbing my heart out. I couldn't believe that, only a week ago, I was in the arms of

Jim in Magna and now, seven days later, I was in what truly felt like a scene from "Oliver Twist".

My door creaked open.

I looked up to see one of the lads from downstairs staring right at me.

"What the fuck are you looking at, poofter?" he snarled.

"I wasn't," I stuttered.

No sooner had I answered than he flew over to my case and started to throw it around the room.

"What you got in here then?" he laughed.

"Just some clothes," I answered.

"Just some clothes," he mimicked in a high-pitched voice.

SMACK.

He thumped me so hard across the back of my head that I almost choked on my tongue.

"Aaaaarrgh!" I screamed.

He pulled the back of my tee shirt and dragged me towards him.

"Tell anyone and you're fucking dead. Got it!" he growled.

"Let me go please!" I pleaded.

"Fucking poof," he said laughing, as he left the room as quickly as he'd entered it.

I held the back of my head, as the sting worsened.

"I HATE ME!" I screamed out loud as I slumped to the floor punching it with as much energy as I had left. David came bursting through the door.

"What's all the shouting!" he said looking at me. Immediately, he realised that something was wrong.

"What is it? What's happened?" he asked crouching down towards me.

"I've just been punched on the back of the head!" I sobbed.

"Who did it?" he demanded.

"One of them lads," I answered.

Just then the lad who had done it came into the room.

"It was HIM!" I shouted.

"What's happened?" he said pretending to not know.

"As if you don't know, Tommy," David answered.

I soon realised, after my third beating from Tommy, that 'grassing' was not the done thing. The more you 'grass' then the harder the beating.

I became more and more withdrawn as the days and weeks went past. I didn't fit in with any of the other kids. David became my rock and, the more time I spent with him, the closer we became. I hated it when he wasn't working. On his days off, I would sit in my room, staring out of the window, watching yet another day passing me by.

When David was on sleepover duty, all the boys were allowed to sit in his room, until midnight, talking. I never did much talking; I would just sit and admire David. I think I had a crush on him and it was driving me insane. As soon as a guy showed me any kind of attention, I would cling onto him like a leech. David was 6ft 4 inches tall with jet-black hair, was quite muscular and had a really warm smile, which made his face all the more attractive. Just before we were sent up to the dorm that night he took me aside.

"When I send you off to bed at twelve, don't fall asleep," he whispered. "Why not?" I asked. "I want to spend some time with you and get to know the real you. I know that you don't like chatting when the other lads are there," he explained.

He was right. I was so shy in front of the others. I realise, now, that it had to do with my low self-esteem, but at the time, I did not have the luxury of analysing it in that way.

"O.K." I answered.

My smile stretched from ear to ear. I couldn't believe that he wanted to get to know me better. If it hadn't been for him, I would have had nothing to look forward to. When we were called to let us know that it was time to go up to bed, butterflies ran riot in my stomach. All of a sudden, I felt really nervous.

I made my way to David's room where the rest of them were already sitting. I began to blush, my face turning redder by the second. Throughout those two hours, I would look over at David to steal a glance at him while the rest weren't looking. Each time I looked over, my eyes would be met with his staring back at me. My heart was racing. Surely he didn't fancy me? He couldn't. It was more than his job was worth. Suddenly, while I was deep in thought, he spoke.

"Right, lads, it's time for some sleep," he said to us all.

As we were leaving the room, he looked at me and winked.

"Night," I said, blushing.

I went to my room as planned and waited in anticipation. After only a short time, my bedroom door opened slowly.

"Hey," he whispered.

"Hey," I whispered back.

He took my arm and led me, silently, on tip-toes, to his room.

"I want a hug from you," he said, as he gently pulled me towards him.

I pressed my head lightly against his chest.

Within minutes, we were all over each other, touching and kissing. I felt so safe in his arms. We didn't have sex; I just lay on his chest for what felt like only minutes, although, in reality, it was hours. At four a.m. I had to go back to my own room, as we both knew that I could never spend a full night in his.

Lying in my bed, I began to cry. I don't know why, to be honest, but my emotions were all over the place. I felt such a huge feeling of loss as I lay there, alone, staring up at the badly-cracked ceiling. My life had taken so many twists and turns in such a short space of time. I didn't want to be gay and I did start to wonder: if the abuse in London hadn't happened, then would I just be 'normal'?

How is it possible for anyone to know what they, truly, are - if their first experience of sex is rape? I hated to think that I would never have the luxury of going on a first date or falling in love with a woman. All I knew was that I had learned, in order to get my own way with men and in order for them to show me some attention, I had to let them have sex with me. Even just being with David, lying naked with him for a few hours, left my heart and soul feeling unclean; yet I didn't even have the courage to say no for the next three weeks. We never had sex at all in those three weeks and, ironically, that really messed up my head: guys who wanted to know me had always wanted sex.

What was he trying to do to me?

He didn't really like me, did he?

He just felt sorry for me; could he not find it in himself to tell me I was unattractive? Rather than say anything, would he just do it as a chore? All these questions of doubt played around in my mind, leaving me with such a deep feeling of sadness. I began to slip into that huge, black hole again. My mind was on a downwards spiral, yet I still let him hold me each night because I felt weak and felt the need for attention. I would enjoy the attention at the time, yet, at the same time, I knew it was destroying me.

What was our connection? Where was this going?

Christmas was approaching fast and this would be the first time I had been away from Kirkby Willows. Christmas had seemed the only normal time in that house. Jim and Enid would always be in high spirits for the festive season, so those times were some of the few happy memories I had and now, here I was, in a prison surrounded by lads who hated me and who, at any given opportunity, would beat me up.

"Three days to go!" Miss Shields shouted down the corridor.

"Can't wait," I muttered under my breath to my 'other' me. I wandered up to my bedroom as I felt my mood grow darker.

Sheer frustration began to rock my brain to the point of explosion.

"I JUST WANT TO BE NORMAL!" I screamed at the top of my voice, with feelings of complete hatred towards myself. My bedroom door flew open.

"What's wrong?" said the voice.

I looked up in shock, as the voice I'd heard was a female one - and this was the male dormitory.

"What you doing here?" I demanded, looking at one of the girls who I recognised as Claire.

"I heard you, from the girl's dorm, screaming and was just checking what the noise was," she replied.

"I was just messing about," I muttered, slightly embarrassed.

"Didn't sound like it to me," she answered.

"Leave me alone anyway," I snapped.

"There's no need to be so snotty; we're not all nasty in here, you know," she replied sharply.

She moved over to my bed and sat down. I moved away from her, slightly, as I felt that her presence was putting me a little on edge. I had been learning quickly that being suspicious of people wasn't always a bad thing. However, she did seem genuine, as she asked me why I was in Croft House and not in another home. We chatted for about five minutes and then, smiling, she asked me a strange question.

"Can you keep secrets?"

"I think so," I answered. I'd kept my rape a secret so far, so, if that counted, then the answer would be yes.

"There's going to be a fire here," she whispered to me.

"A fire?" I replied with a look of confusion on my face.

"Yeah! How exciting is that!" she squealed, in a high-pitched, animated voice.

I was completely lost at this point. I didn't have a clue what she was talking about - or even why she was telling me.

"On New Year's Eve, all the girls are going to burn this shit hole down," she said calmly.

"What!" I exclaimed as my eyes widened in disbelief.

"How cool is that! We'll all have to get moved to a nicer place if this one isn't here any more," she replied.

This sounded like an AMAZING idea! I'd be able to escape the bullies at last. My mind began to wander as I thought of the scene in which I'm saying goodbye to David. How I wished he would love me and like me.

Suddenly, my attention was brought back to my room as David walked in.

"Claire, what are you doing in here?" he asked.

"Sorry, Dave! I just came to check Leon was o.k. Isn't that right, Leon?" she said, looking at me to get her off the hook.

"Yeah," I answered with a painted-on smile.

"Well, you know you shouldn't be in here. Go on, back to your own side," he ordered.

"Tell anyone about what I said and you're dead," she whispered to me as she ran out of the room.

"Tell anyone what?" Dave asked me directly.

"Oh nothing; she was just telling me stuff about her family," I lied.

I couldn't tell him even if I wanted to. At the end of the day he was one of 'them'. I'd already had a battering for being a 'grass'. I didn't have the energy to get into another fight. Why had she told me that they were going to do it anyway? Did she really like me or was it just another one of those cruel tricks where I'm the bait?

I had a plan.

"Will it work?" I whispered to my 'other' me.

Only time would tell.

They next few days I spent my time hatching a foolproof plan. I was so messed- up, emotionally, at that point and, when that happens, you just don't think straight. Desperation kicks in on a high level and your thoughts become completely irrational.

In my head, I calculated that, if the fire happened and the place burned down, we would all have to be moved. I knew already that there was no room in the other homes as that's why I was here in the first place. Therefore, all the kids who had to be under supervision would have to be placed in some sort of care. After the fire, we would all be quizzed by the police and at that point I could 'grass' on the people involved and then I would need to be protected. David would surely protect me, wouldn't he? I could go and stay with him, couldn't I? There wouldn't be anywhere else for me to go and I could suggest that my support worker look after me.

"Perfect!" I whispered to myself; but, also, out loud in excitement.

Christmas day was so dull. The only good thing was that there weren't many kids in over that weekend as most of them had gone away on home leave. Due to the fact that I didn't have a home to go to, I was left with the ones who weren't allowed out of the building, whether they had a home or not. In total, there were four of us left behind. I missed Kirkby Willows that day and I missed my sister. We'd had no contact for weeks now and today just magnified how lonely I was.

David wouldn't be in until later as he was visiting his parents with his girlfriend. I was so jealous of him having someone else. I'd only found out last week that he even had a girlfriend. When I'd asked him about it he said that his life outside of work was a different subject and shouldn't be discussed. How could I not discuss it! Each time I lay with him I would pry more and more into his personal life. It became an obsession. I began to think that, maybe, if the place was torched then my plan would work and we would be together; then he would feel differently about me.

Of course, I know, now, that this was my mind being completely irrational.

As the weekend came to an end, so did the quiet, as all the kids began pouring back through the doors with their fancy presents and tales of family fun. I felt so bitter and jealous towards them. Why couldn't I have had a normal family? I wouldn't have had to run away and I wouldn't be in this living hell.

I waited impatiently for Claire returning and, as soon as she did, I pounced on her.

"When is this fire gonna happen then?" I whispered.

"I've told you! New Years Eve," she snapped.

"I just wanted to make sure it was still happening that's all" I snapped back.

I was desperate for my plan to work.

It had to work.

In the lead up to New Year's Eve, I couldn't sleep for worry. This was my chance to get my life sorted out and be happy. It was all going to work as long as this fire plan went ahead. Time after time, I would check with Claire just to make sure nothing had changed. She grew so sick and tired of me badgering her about it.

"Shut the fuck up about it. You're gonna get us caught!" she snarled.

"How will I?" I snapped back. I had everything to lose if this fell through.

"Because you ask so many times someone is going to hear you!" she said more calmly.

"Sorry. I'm just excited, that's all", I lied.

It was New Year's Eve soon enough. We were all told that there would be a party in the main television room and we would be given party food and loud music, along with two cans of beer each.

"Nice one!" David shrieked. He was a pure beer monster if ever I'd seen one.

"But I'm warning you all. Any trouble or messing about and the whole thing will be cancelled. Do I make myself clear?" Miss. Shields warned.

"Yes, Miss," we all answered.

We all knew that there would be no messing about that night. We would all be on our best behaviour. If we weren't, then the whole plan would be ruined.

The night was beginning to draw to an end and we were all in high spirits.

"It's almost twelve 'o' clock!" Miss Shields screamed.

"Quickly! Everyone join hands," David added. Laughter echoed into every corner of the room.

Blackout.

"Open the door…. somebody… HELP…Open the door," screams a
voice.

For a moment, I'm confused. I don't know where I am. I try to focus on the door in front of me, but my eyes feel swollen. They sting as I try to open them. I'm scared. I feel like I'm going blind. There is a haze in front of me. Why is it so dark? What's happening? The screams are growing louder. There is a thumping noise coming from behind the door.

Burning. I can smell burning.

Someone shouts, "Leon", as I still find it hard to focus.

"Leon!" the voice shouts again. I start to cough and my insides feel like
they are on fire…Fire…. FIRE. I can smell burning. Smoke and flames lick up the crack at the base of the door.

"OH MY GOD!" I scream as my brain clicks like the clog of a large wheel.

"Leon!" screams the familiar voice. It's David. Why can't I see him?

I feel an arm shaking my side.

"What's happening?" I scream.

"Please, Leon. We have to get out," David shrieks, as his grip becomes firmer than ever.

Quickly, I scramble to my feet. Still completely naked I begin to scurry around for my clothes. The flames creep even further up the base of the door.

"There's a fire…Come on…Get dressed!" David screams.

" I'm trying!" I scream back, shaking with fear.

"We need to get out of here!" he shouts.

"They've done it. They've set the place on fire," I scream back.

"What are you talking about?" David demands.

My breathing becomes more and more irregular as the seconds tick by. The screams from behind the door have gone.

I panic.

"We're going to die, aren't we?" I ask as I choke. Tears are streaming down my face, as the smoke fills my lungs. David tries, frantically, to drench a hand towel in the hand basin.

"Give me a hand, Leon. We don't have much time," he shouts.

"Please, God. Don't let me die. Not like this!" I scream as I fumble about, trying to turn the taps on as much as they will go. David throws the towel towards the bottom of the door, as I fill the coffee cup with more water to kill the flames that are now half-way up the door. The flames make a hissing noise, as the flames turn to black, sooty smoke. The walls and windows are now all a black haze. We manage to kill the flames and David, quickly, stuffs the towel into the crack under the door to stop the flames.

"Take off your clothes…QUICKLY! All of them!" he screams.

"WHAT!" I shriek.

"Take them all off!" he repeats.

Without even asking why again, I begin to tear my clothes off, buttons flying off as I did so.

"Soak them under the tap. Get them drenched," he orders.

As I start to soak them, David copies me.

"Now, put them back on and cover yourself as best as you can," he demands. Without questioning, I do as he tells me. Ironically, the ice cold water burns my skin. I'm shaking with a mixture of cold and fright.

"When I open this door we are going to run… don't stop…. Just keep running and make your way down the stairs and out through the fire door at the shower block…It's our nearest exit," he explains with great panic in his voice.

"What about you?" I scream.

"I need to check everyone is out of the building… Promise me you will do as I say, Leon," he begs.

"What if we can't get out and we're trapped?" I scream.

"Just do as I say and you'll be O.K!" he screams back.

At that moment, panic takes over my whole body. I have never been so frightened of dying as I was there and then. I decide to lift the chair next to the desk and try to hurl it through the window.

"NO!" David shouts as he drags me back.

"We're going to burn to death!" I exclaim as, desperately, I try to lunge back towards the window.

"If you smash the window the flames will come back even worse than before!" he shouts at me.

I fall to the floor, choking from the deadly fumes. David drags me to my feet.

"I'm going to open the door…Remember to do as I said!" he shouts.

Suddenly, he pulls the door open and all we can see in front of us are smoke and flames. Fear grips every part of my body. I stiffen with fright.

"RUN!" David screams.

Without giving it a second thought, I run through the thick smoke. I can't see anything in front of me, but black smog and bright orange flames. I use my hands to guide me, stretching my fingers beyond their capability and stumbling into the unknown. I don't even know which part of the building I am in. Desperately, I try to focus, as I struggle to breathe.

Is this the end?

Why didn't I tell David what was planned?

All these questions haze my thoughts until one single thought flashes into my head like a bolt of lightening.

"I DON'T WANT TO DIE!" I scream out loud as my mind snaps into focus.

I won't be beaten!

Not like this.

Never!

As I struggle down the long corridor, trying desperately to avoid the flames, I see a shadow in front of me.

"Who's there...? Please help me," says the weakened voice.

I recognise the voice. It's Lisa: one of the girls who was part of the group planning to start the fire. Why was she still in the building? Surely they had all got out first.

"Where is everyone?" I shout to her, as I get closer.

"I don't know, but we need to get out fast!" she shouts back.

We take each other's hands and race through the corridor and almost fall head-over-heels down the staircase. I do exactly as David told me and head towards the shower block but, just as we turn the corner to go, we are halted by a huge banging noise. It rips through the corridor like a huge bolt of thunder. I feel the floor move from underneath where we are standing.

"What the fuck was that!" Lisa screams.

"I don't know! Let's get out of here!" I scream back. Just then David appears carrying Dawn.

"Come on! The whole building is gonna go up!" David shrieks.

We run for the shower block door and scramble through it like a herd of frightened animals.

As we reach the clean air outside, we are surrounded by blue lights, people wandering around aimlessly, the sound of screams, the sound of crying. I feel as though a scene from a horror film is unfolding right in front of us.

"What have you done!"? I scream at Lisa as I shake her uncontrollably.

She grasps her hair in despair, clutching at it like a wild cat desperate to hold on to its prey.

"Shut it! Shut it!" she repeats over and over as her body rocks back and forth.

The memory of that night will haunt my dreams for a lifetime. It made me realise that from a single stupid action being carried out, lives were almost lost. I felt complete and utter disgust to think that I had been a part of this. I might not have been the one who had struck the match and started this carnage, but I was as much a part to blame as the ones who had done so.

We were all taken to hospital that night. Most had suffered smoke inhalation while the less fortunate ones, like Dawn, suffered much worse injuries. Her legs would be scarred for life. The Christmas tree, which was torched and had started the fire, had collapsed on top of her within seconds of lighting it, falling onto her legs with no mercy. She was lucky to be alive.

We all were.

Life is something we all take for granted and some people never fully appreciate it, even after such events.

I include myself in that.

My first brush with death would become the first one of four.

The following day, after the fire, we were all taken to the police station for questioning. Each of us took it in turn to be interviewed. I was still convinced that my plan was going to work at that point but, as the day unfolded, I soon realised I would have to take desperate measures to seal the deal. As part of the home had been untouched by the fire, other than smoke damage, we were informed that we would be going back there once we had finished at the station. The questioning came to an end and we all gave the same answer to the police. We knew nothing.

The day drew to a close and we were taken back to the hellhole. Almost immediately upon our arrival, David was taken into the office. He seemed to be away for hours. On his return, he looked broken.

"Are you O.K?" I asked with concern.

"No I'm not," he snapped.

"What's wrong?" I asked.

"I'm facing the sack for this fire!" he snapped.

"What?"

"They are saying the door wasn't locked and that, if it had been, then none of this could have happened. I know for a fact I locked it. I just don't understand." He looked genuinely shocked.

It transpired that David had been accused of not locking the door leading to the bottom corridor. I knew that the girls had taken the key earlier and had it copied. He HAD actually locked it. This whole thing was a mess and I couldn't believe that the one person I cared about was being hurt the most. I had to think quickly.

"David!" I said, looking straight at him.

"What is it, Leon? You look worried now," he replied with concern.

"I need to tell you something," I said, as my heart rate started to speed up.

"What?"

"Can we go somewhere private?" I asked.

"Sure," he replied, taking my arm to manoeuvre me to a quiet part of the room.

"What's going to happen to happen to all of us?" I asked nervously.

"Well, we know someone started the fire on purpose because, whoever it was, turned the alarms off before they started it," he stated.

"They turned them off!" I gasped. My eyes were bulging with fear. Claire hadn't said anything about that in the plan. It was just supposed to cause enough damage to get us all moved. They must have known when they switched the alarms off that it might cause deaths. I'd been part of this. If I'd told David earlier, it would never have come to this in the first place.

"Is there something you want to tell me, Leon?" he asked.

Without even taking in a breath, I answered him.

"I know who it was", I said, still shaking with the shock of what he was telling me.

"WHAT!" he hissed.

"I know who it was," I repeated.

"Who? And why didn't you say earlier?" he added.

"I was scared to say anything at the time and I thought that maybe if I did I would get into trouble as well," I blurted out.

I figured now that if I gave the police the names of the culprits I would have to be taken away for my own protection.

"If I tell you, can I come and stay with you?" I added.

"Stay where?" he asked.

"At your place; it'll be too dangerous to stay here if I do tell you," I answered.

At this point David must have realised that if he agreed to what I was saying, he would get the information out of me. His job was on the line.

"Tell me and I'll see what I can do," he said.

At that very moment, I actually believed what he was saying. My mind was all over the place and, once again, all I wanted or cared about was to be with David and for him to like me and want me. Of course, he just wanted to save his job. We were both in desperate situations, for different reasons. After telling David everything I knew, I was taken into the main office and had to repeat my story to the governor.

"You idiot!" snarled Mr. Lanson.

He was a strong and solid, tall man who would put the fear of God in you without even opening his mouth. I was petrified as I repeated my story to him.

"BRING THEM IN NOW!" he screamed to the senior staff, all of whom had just listened to my story.

No sooner had I finished what I was saying - and the three members of staff had rushed from the office - than, within minutes, there was a commotion in the corridor outside.

"I'll fucking stab you, Leon!" Claire screamed.

The fear I felt right there in that room was one I'd never quite experienced before; even after all the incidents in London, I was petrified.

To hear someone threaten you in that way makes you feel sick to the pit of your stomach. Where was my life going? Was this all I was ever going to experience?

Abuse.

Threats.

Hatred.

The girls were taken to the police station and charged with arson. To this day I have never seen them again. Nor do I want to.

"Right, Leon," snapped Mr. Lanson. I looked at him sheepishly. I guessed that if I'd told about the plan earlier I would have been beaten up, but now it was much worse all round.

David was facing the sack, Dawn had been nearly burnt to death, we were all lucky to be alive, yet now my life was under threat for 'grassing'.

"You're going to be moved," he added.

I looked at David for his support. Surely he would say that I could go with him and that he would look after me and protect me from harm.

Wouldn't he?

Couldn't he?

He just lowered his head towards the ground and dismissed the fear on my face.

I was pathetic: a useless piece of shit; Jim and Enid's doormat for eternity. I almost wished I was back there, away from this world of crime in which I was becoming involved. I felt sick to the pit of my stomach. Everything and everybody with whom I came into contact turned to poison.

"Where?" I whispered.

"Back to where you belong," he hissed.

"WHAT!" I screamed.

Suddenly, fear gripped my body tighter than ever before. I hadn't really meant that I wanted to be back in Kirkby Willows.

Why is it only bad wishes come true?

"To a place called Hill View. Go and pack your things," he added.

"But why?" I asked.

"I thought you'd be pleased. It saves getting stabbed here," he said with a familiar smirk on his face.

I went upstairs and began to pack together my belongings. Tears started to roll down my face. It is a living hell being somewhere you hate, yet also hating leaving it, to go somewhere else new.

"It's going to be O.K." David said, as he helped me pack.

"It's not though. I only did it to be with you. You hate me, don't you," I cried.

"Hey, come on. I don't hate you, Leon. You made a mistake by not telling anyone what you knew; but I don't hate you," he said with a soft voice.

After we had packed, David took me to his car for the two-hour drive. I looked behind into the rear window of the car as the sun was setting over Canton. Again I felt lost, I felt broken, heart crushed, soul destroyed. Moving on again because I'd messed up at yet another place where I was staying.

"Am I ever going to see you again?" I cried.

"Of course you are. Nothing is forever," he said, touching my leg, as though for comfort.

I didn't believe him. Why should I? No-one else had ever kept their promises, and the rate at which people were coming and going, in and out of my life, was becoming faster and faster.

I wanted to die.

I never settled at Hill View. It was like a country home in the middle of nowhere. Whenever you did something wrong, you were made to stand at the top of the landing, on the spot, for up to three hours, after which you were taken downstairs and made to apologise to the rest of the kids and staff for your bad behaviour. On top of that, everyone would lose their privileges for a whole week. It wasn't so bad if you got into trouble when there was a few of you, but if you got into trouble alone, then you would feel like a complete outcast. This was their way of controlling us. If you tried to run away, all of your footwear would be confiscated and you would have to sign your shoes in and out whenever you went anywhere escorted with a staff member.

I was sent back to my old school, which was about an hour's drive each day. The only saving grace was being reunited with my old friend, Anthony Sharpe. I had really missed him over those few months of being in Canton, but not even that friendship would keep me there. The weeks turned into months and I became more and more withdrawn. I didn't belong anywhere.

My self-hatred was taking on a new twist. I began to dismiss mirrors, refusing to look at the reflection I so hated. Looking in the mirror at myself only made me feel sick. Some days, I would decide I was too fat and, other days, too skinny. I realise, now, years later, that it was all to do with my inner self-loathing. The mind is a powerful foe. I would do anything to make myself feel worse, because I felt that my existence in this world was simply to be punished. Food became my enemy and I would use it as a weapon to destroy myself. It was a way of punishing my own self for being such a piece of trash.

I started to force sharp objects up my anal passage to hurt myself. This began to be my nightly ritual when it was lights out at bedtime. I would choose the object I was going to use after tea each night and, then, I would sneak it up to my room and hide it under my pillow for later that evening. I used a fork most nights, as that was the most painful implement and would cause bleeding. I would get such satisfaction from cutting the passage, especially the times where I was really rough and drew blood from the sharp prongs. I just wanted to cause myself as much damage as I could. Hitting myself on the back of the head, pulling my hair roughly, nipping myself, anything to stamp out the pain of the way I felt inside. I was at the stage where I wanted to be abused. I began to think about the time I'd spent in London and the things that had happened to me while I was away. The bad memories didn't seem so bad anymore: at least then I had been getting attention. Of course, this was simply my way of dealing with the abuse. When you hate yourself as much as I did, no amount of pain you can cause yourself will take it away.

One day, while at school, I decided that it was time to move on again. I thought that if I ran away and visited my foster-auntie, Imogen, who was Enid's sister, she would help. She was my only hope. I didn't really know her very well, but had visited her a few times while staying in Canton. She had been more than welcoming and had made it clear that any differences between her Enid and me were irrelevant. She wasn't aware of what had gone on at Kirkby Willows at this point.

The school bell had just gone and I knew that the time to go was now or never. I would be picked up in half an hour by taxi to take me on the one-hour drive back to Hill View. In total, that would give me one and a half hours to get on my way. I had the fifteen pounds taxi fare that I could use to get a bus or a train to Canton.

I ran really fast to the bus station - and didn't look behind me once. I decided that the bus would be cheaper than the train. Even when they did realise that I wouldn't be returning that night, I would be long gone and they wouldn't know of my whereabouts anyway.

I reached the bus station and went to buy my ticket. The fare cost more than the money I had and so the farthest I would be able to travel was the town before Canton, called Pendal.

"Shit!" I hissed to myself.

"What's that, lad?" said the guy behind the counter at the ticket office.

"Er…nothing…. I was just talking to myself" I replied.

"So do you want the ticket?" he snapped.

"Yes, please," I answered.

Sweat started to trickle down my face as I began stressing about the gap left in my proposed journey. However, I figured that once I was on the bus I would pretend to be asleep just before we got to Pendal and then, that way, I could stay on for the whole journey. As the bus pulled away, I started to panic. What was I doing? All I ever did was run from one place to the next, time after time. My life was an absolute joke.

I dozed on and off as the gentle rocking of the bus made me sleepy. As we drew closer to Pendal I started to fidget and my adrenalin kicked in making my heart feel as though it was going to squeeze through my school jumper.

"Last stop before Canton," the ticket collector shouted.

This was it! It was time to get my acting skills into full swing. Quickly, I squeezed my eyes closed and hoped I would go unnoticed. The ticket collector clocked what I was up to and came over almost immediately.

"Oi. I called the Pendal stop," he snapped.

I pretended to wake up slowly as if having been in a deep sleep.

"Wh…. what?" I said with a sleepy voice.

"Save the dramatics, lad. I know what you're up to. Now clear off before the police get involved," he snapped again.

I didn't need to be told twice. The last thing I needed was a commotion and the police becoming involved.

It had been worth the try.

"Shit! Shit! Shit!" I repeated over and over.

It was so dark now. The moon was out and the daylight had long gone. I stood at the roadside and began to cry. Yet again, I felt the feeling of complete failure. My life was on a constant decline: running from one place to the next, just me with my 'other' me for company. I was tired of the constant struggle to keep my mind from dying. My heart seemed to have died long ago, along with my soul.

It was hard ever to imagine life feeling any other way. This was all I knew. I never gave up on the dream that there I was someone out there who wanted to love me, take care of me, hold me and touch me with love and kindness. I've watched clouds brush past the sun and then clear again to reveal a deep blue sky full of nothing other than the sun which makes it alive. That's what I wanted to feel: alive.

After pausing for a while and wiping away the tears, I started my seventeen-mile walk to Canton. I don't know what it is that gives a person the energy to carry on because, when you feel like your life is a black cloud, what is it that stops you giving in? What makes you breathe and what makes you take each step? It was almost as though my legs were in autopilot, thinking on their own, taking on their own adventure, because my body was too weak to go on.

It took me almost four hours before I could see the bright lights of Canton in front of me. It was a sight I was only too happy to see. I wondered if David would be happy to see me? I was tempted to look for him, but was scared he would hand me in to the police.

I never quite understood on what level our relationship had existed. He had never tried to touch me in a sexual way, yet we had lain naked together many nights and kissed intimately more often than not. He held a special place in my mind, where no-one could touch it, along with my memories of Jim, from Magna. It felt like my time in Liverpool was just another faded memory.

I have come to accept that some things in life never do become clear.

My feet were swollen and blistered from the long walk and I started to panic as I drew further into town and closer to Tarnside which was the area where my auntie Imogen lived. What if she turned me away? What then? She was my only hope.

I reached the gate, which led to her house and, for a second, turned away to double back on my steps. My self-doubt was going to make me change my mind.

"You've come this far", I whispered to my 'other' me.

I knocked at the door and, seconds later, the hall light lit up outside to reveal a large moth fluttering around the dusty bulb casing.

The door opened. It was my auntie.

"Leon!" she exclaimed with surprise.

"Hiya…can I…can I come in?" I asked, with a shaky uncertainty in my voice.

"Of course you can! Give me a hug," she said, holding her arms out. Immediately, I burst into a flood of tears.

"I've run away from Hill View," I said, snivelling through the tears.

"I know. They've been on the phone to ask if you'd turned up here," she explained.

"Please don't call them," I whispered.

"Don't worry about that now. Come on in. We can sit down and you can tell me what's happened," she replied.

"Thank you! Thank you so much!" I felt such overwhelming relief.

We went inside and she made me a strong cup of coffee and some cheese and pickle sandwiches, which I wolfed down within minutes. I had been hungry since I'd boarded the bus, but the fare had left me with no money for even a carton of juice, let alone some food. I chatted to her for hours about Hill View.

"I can't go back. I hate it!" I told her.

"Why don't I phone Penny in the morning and let her know you're safe," she answered.

"What if she sends me back?" I could hear the panic in my own voice.

"It's o.k. If there's a problem, then you can stay here until it's sorted."

"Really?" I exclaimed, with excitement.

"Really!" she answered, giving me another hug.

I never disclosed anything else at that point about Kirkby Willows or London. I still wasn't ready to open that can of worms. It would happen very shortly, however.

The next morning, my auntie phoned Penny to let her know I was o.k. and they arranged that I could stay with her for a few days until we had a meeting with the people from Hill View. It was agreed that this meeting would take place in Canton.

My few days at my auntie's were good ones. Although I was still very "down", she would try to cheer me up at any given opportunity. I didn't do much for those days, other than watch television and chat about anything and everything. It was a lovely, warm sensation being able to talk without feeling threatened. I also slept a little better, but I would still self-harm once she'd gone to bed. My self-loathing hadn't stopped there. I doubted, then, that it ever would.

The day of the meeting arrived and I was really nervous. I had what I can only describe as a floating feeling in my stomach; the same feeling you get when you've been caught for doing something wrong. Not like butterflies, but worse. At the meeting I received an enormous surprise.

"David!" I screamed as I walked into the room full of both familiar and unfamiliar faces. He came straight over and gave me a huge hug, which felt amazing. He was there as a representative for Croft House. Also there was Steve from Hill View, my social worker Penny, my auntie Imogen and a few others who I didn't know. The meeting was to try and come up with a clearer picture as to why I was running away so much. I tried to explain that I hated Hill View, it was too much going back to a school from my past and I wanted to be in Canton to build up on a broken rapport with my sister, Beverly. My auntie had helped me with what I wanted to say.

"We just find he is too over-sensitive," Steve, from Hill View, interrupted.

"How DARE you fault him for being over-sensitive. Don't you think, putting yourself in his situation for just one minute that YOU would be just even a little over-sensitive!" my auntie snapped.

"Now just a minute," he snapped back.

"O.K! We won't get anywhere like this. Imogen, could you take Leon to the juice machine in the hallway and we will have five minutes to reach a decision on the facts we've heard today," Penny said.

"Sure," my auntie replied.

"O.K. Leon, love?" asked Penny.

"Yeah!" I answered, solemn-faced.

"Good. We'll be as quick as possible," she replied.

So that was it. My future was about to be decided without me even being present! At least I'd had my say this time, though, before a decision had been made. It wasn't long before we were called back into the room.

" O.K. We've reached a decision" Penny announced.

My heart started to pound harder and harder as the seconds went by.

"Please don't send me back to Hill View!" I cried with panic.

"You're not going back to Hill View. It's been decided that, for your well-being, you will now move to Westline Road," she explained.

"With Beverly!" I screamed, not daring to believe it for one single minute.

"Well, Beverly has just moved out, which is why there is now a space available. But we are going to ensure that you are both in close contact from now on" she explained.

"Thank you!" I screamed.

Tears ran down my face as I hugged Penny, my auntie and David in turns. I wasn't going to Croft House, I wasn't going back to Hill View, I was going to a residential home AND I was going to see my sister. If it hadn't been for the help of my foster auntie, the meeting could never have happened. For that, I am forever grateful.

That very afternoon I moved into what was going to be my new home. My auntie came along with Penny and myself - for support. When we arrived, I was introduced to the staff and the house head, Miss Shrill. I had met her at Croft House the year before. It was more like a normal house than any I'd stayed in previously. After a brief meeting, Penny and my auntie left and I settled in.

There was a living room and dining area, a large kitchen, a study room, three bathrooms and eight bedrooms. Joined on via a corridor was another house. This was called the independent unit where, once you were almost sixteen, you'd receive training on how to live on your own.

I spent my first few days becoming familiar with my new surroundings and meeting the other six kids. They were all older than me, apart from Grant and Tina who were thirteen, and Jack who was twelve. I shared a bedroom with Jack. We both got on really well. It was great to have a little pal with whom I could just chat, normally. Tina really caught my eye. I thought she was so beautiful with her dark hair and olive skin. She looked very Italian. Over the weeks, we became closer and closer. One of the older girls, Julie, had a steady boyfriend and she encouraged Tina and me to start dating. Were my prayers finally becoming a reality? We kissed on many occasions and I felt really comfortable with her. The more time we spent together, the more inseparable we became. She made me laugh so much; I never remembered ever feeling this happy. Of course my issues were still there under the surface yet, when I was with her, I would forget about most of them.

Also, I had been reunited with my sister at this point. It felt so strange seeing her after such a long time. She was different. She had moved into a bed-sit in the town centre and was seeing a guy called Neil. He was very manly and I remember feeling slightly threatened by him. His personality and character made me feel uneasy when I was around him. However, my sister was completely besotted, so I always made the effort when I went to visit her, as he was constantly there. I was happy that we were reunited yet, at the same time, I never fully had her back because now I had to share her. The one person who was part of me in this whole world and I had to share her. Our relationship never really gelled and that hurt. I had believed that, once we were back together again, it would just be her and me against the world.

My priorities began to change and that is when I clung on to Tina even more. I soon started to realise that it was a mother-figure I was pining for as, in my eyes, Beverly was my guardian. She was my older sister, my protector, even though, in our younger years, she was the quieter one. That had now changed. After all the experiences I had gone through over the last year, I was left with deep-rooted emotional issues which could only be sorted by making other people aware of them. But I couldn't. I was still too ashamed of what had gone on. I needed looked after and had hoped that my sister was going to be the one to do it. However, through no fault of her own, she had someone else, now: someone who was taking care of her, just as I wanted her to take care of me.

It was at that point that I began to grow obsessed with the idea that, just like magic, my natural mother was going to turn up out of the blue and take me in her arms, wash away all of the pain and hurt I had endured over the last fifteen years and make everything all right. Three years earlier, when I'd been in Ramsey Road children's home I had begged my social worker, Irene, to help me track my natural mother. She had promised to help me. Yet again, another social worker had taken over my case and those promises left faster than she did.

Tina became my life. I completely lost myself in her. I only ever wanted to be in her company and everyone else around me faded into the background. Rightly or wrongly, I would cling on to one person at a time. Multiple friendships never worked for me. An aspect of my personality, and my lack of social skills, which demonstrated itself in such a way that, whenever I would meet someone or become intimate with them, I would hold on tight to them because I didn't want to share them with anyone else. Loss would mean heartache and loneliness.

Julie had been moved into the independent unit by now, as she was due to leave in a few months to start her new life out of care. Tina and I would have to sneak next door to see her, as we weren't supposed to go into the unit without supervision. One day, while on one of our sneaky visits, I was talking to Mick, Julie's boyfriend, and the one conversation I had dreaded the most came up.

"How many girls have you shagged then?" he asked me in a very direct manner.

"How do you mean?" I answered, embarrassed.

What did I think he meant! There only was one way of asking if you were a virgin and he had just asked it!

"Er…. well…" I stuttered.

"Don't be shy, mate!" he shrieked with a huge grin on his face.

The colour of my face crimsoned to a shade darker than scarlet.

"Well…I'm…. I've…." I continued to stutter.

"You're the big V aren't you!" he giggled.

I was so embarrassed. The thought of sleeping with a girl terrified me. I didn't even know what I was supposed to do! I was a virgin in that sense, or, as he called it, the big V!

"Er…yes," I answered, awkwardly.

I had to tell the truth. It was too obvious anyway. He would have seen right through it and would have ridiculed me if I'd lied. At that moment, Julie came running into the kitchen where we were standing. She had the widest smile drawn across her face and looked more like a caricature from a Disney film.

"Well?" she asked looking at Mick.

"Yep" he answered with a grin.

"I knew it!" she shrieked.

"What?" I asked.

"You're both virgins!" she screamed.

While Mick had been questioning me, Julie had been asking Tina the same. Tina peered round the side of the kitchen door looking even more embarrassed than I did.

"Come on. Don't be shy. You're both in the same boat," Julie giggled as she took Tina's arm. I walked over to Tina and wrapped my arms around her.

"I'm so embarrassed," I whispered into her ear.

"Me too," she whispered back.

We hugged some more and tried to laugh off the situation that we'd been put in. Suddenly, Julie spoke.

"I've got an idea," she said looking in our direction.

"What?" we both said back to her.

"Do you want to lose your virginity?" she asked smiling.

"I don't know. I'm nervous," Tina replied.

"There's nothing to be nervous about," Julie giggled.

Julie had come up with a great plan for us to spend a few hours together, alone. The only way it would work was if the resident dragon, Mrs. Mason, fell for the story. The four of us agreed to have a miniature dinner party together and then Tina and I would be able to use the spare bedroom upstairs afterwards. I was so nervous, but I knew that, to move forward with my issues about my sexuality, I would need to do it. I adored Tina and figured that we knew each other well enough at least to try sleeping together.

"Let's do it!" I said, nervously turning to Tina.

"Let's!" she replied with a gorgeous smile on her face.

So that was it. We were going to lose our virginity in the independent unit; but first, we had to tell a few white lies to escape hawk-eyed Mrs. Manson.

Mrs. Manson was a complete battle-axe. She loved catching you out at any given opportunity. She was best friends with the larger-than-life cook, Anne. They would sit in the kitchen, for hours, gossiping about anything and everything, cackling like two old witches. She loved nothing more than handing out punishments such as grounding you for being home later than arranged. I must admit I loved winding her up and giving her cheek. It was my way of having a laugh at her expense. The slightest thing would send her into a frenzy of activity and she would scream at the top of her voice. No one ever took her seriously, though. She must have been at least eighty years old and only about 4ft 10". Even Jack, who was only twelve and short for his age, towered over her like a giant.

On one memorable occasion, Grant had been caught stealing a handful of cakes from the larder. It was his turn to get the goodies and he had gone in with a freezer bag to fill it with fancies. No sooner had he filled the bag than hawk-eyed Manson was right there behind him. She would sit in the office listening for the larder door opening, because it made a certain squeaking noise when it was opened. She didn't miss a trick.

"Got you!" she screamed with glee, as she grabbed the back of his jumper.

"Get off me!" Grant had screamed back as he almost jumped out of his skin.

As she pulled his jumper tighter, Grant turned around sharply to escape her grasp and lifted the bag of goodies above his head. As he did so, she jolted forwards and the bag came crashing down on her head, bouncing off her wiry hair and tipping out the contents of the bag as it touched. We all ran in to see the commotion and, as we did, we were faced with her standing there with butter icing, crumbs and chocolate dripping down her face. I have never laughed so much at such a funny sight. Even today it makes me howl with laughter. Needless to say, Grant was grounded for a week!

To con Mrs. Manson, we would need to have a valid story.

"Tomorrow we can say we're going to the cinema, and, instead of getting the bus at the bottom of the road, we can double back on ourselves and come through Julie's back door," I said.

"Sounds like a plan to me," Julie answered.

So there we had it: the big plan to get time alone, without prying eyes watching our every move.

That would give us at least three and a half hours together.

I hardly slept a wink that night. My mind was a mixture of fear, excitement and nerves.

I didn't know the first thing about sleeping with a girl, but I so desperately wanted to experience it.

Tomorrow couldn't come soon enough.

This was the day I would, hopefully, lose my virginity properly. This should be what my first-ever experience of sex should have been like. I wanted to enjoy the night so much. A few hours and I would be lying naked with a girl.

The day went past in a blur as I psyched myself up for the evening. I don't know who was more nervous, Tina or me.

"Right then. Let's go and see Mrs. Manson," I whispered to Tina.

"You do the talking and I'll just look at her the whole time. I can tell by the look on her face if she thinks you're lying or not.

"O.K." I said.

My heart was racing with excitement as we walked up the short corridor towards the office door. I knocked on it loudly.

"What is it!" shrieked the familiar, witch-like voice.

"It's Leon!" I shouted through the thick wood.

"Well, come in!" she snapped.

"Here goes!" I whispered to Tina, giving her a quick kiss on the lips before I opened the door.

She was sitting behind the large table like she was some kind of queen. I found it really hard not to start sniggering. Every time I looked at her these days I couldn't help but visualise the cake incident.

"What is it?" she asked.

"Can we please go to the cinema tonight?" I asked, as sweetly as possible.

"Both of you?" she asked, as she raised herself from the chair.

She had a habit of pacing back and forth while burning holes in you with her old baggy eyes.

"Yes. We should be back by nine-thirty," I said, beginning to stutter.

"Any later and you're grounded!" she snapped.

That was her way of saying 'Yes. Enjoy your film' I guess.

"Thank you!" I said.

"Thank you," Tina added.

We went to head for the door when, suddenly she called us back.

"Just a minute!" she shrieked.

Tina and I looked at one another. We'd been caught out. But how!

"I know what you two are up to" she sneered.

"We're not up to anything," I said.

"So there won't be any kissing in the back row then?" she smiled. I couldn't believe she'd actually smiled. She was human after all!

"Now go on, and don't be late," she said as she made a brushing movement with her hand as if to say "shoo".

As soon as the office door closed we both hugged each other tightly.

"Oh my God. We've done it!" I whispered excitedly.

"Well, what are we waiting for? Let's go!" Tina answered.

We did as we planned and double-backed to the independent unit. Once we reached there, Julie started dishing some pasta out onto plates. Neither of us ate a thing, as we were both too nervous.

"Right then. Get upstairs, the pair of you." Julie said looking at us.

We did as she said and made our way to the bedroom. When we walked in, there was a small packet on the bed.

"What's this?" I asked as I began to open it.

"I asked Julie to get us a condom," Tina answered.

"I've never used one of these before," I said.

"There should be some instructions inside," she answered.

I opened the box, and inside, there was a step-by-step instruction sheet on how to put on the condom. We started to kiss passionately; one thing led to another and, before long, we were both naked. My tongue began to explore the beautiful body that lay in front of me. I felt so at ease with Tina as I kissed and caressed her naked flesh, becoming more and more aroused as each second passed. Two bodies became one as our skin touched closely together. Beads of sweat trickled slowly down my face as our bodies became more heated. I placed the condom on and Tina drew me closer towards her. After a few seconds I had entered her. It felt so right to be doing this. Not once did I sense a feeling of awkwardness. As I moved deeper inside, the passion heightened to a new level. A feeling of complete ecstasy took hold of me. As we both climaxed, screams of passion echoed around the room; but, as I pulled away, Tina screamed.

"I'm bleeding! Why am I bleeding?" she screamed.

"Oh my God!" was all I could say.

Julie raced into the bedroom.

"What's happened? What's wrong?" she shouted.

"I'm bleeding!" Tina cried.

"Calm down," Julie said, as she rushed to be by Tina's side.

"Why has that happened?" I asked Julie as my mind became blank.

"Girls bleed when they do 'it' for the first time. I did," she explained.

"Really?" Tina cried.

"Yes. Go and clean yourself up. You're fine," she said reassuringly.

Rather an anti-climax after a climax!

All the same, I was in total awe of this girl now. I was under her spell. At last I didn't feel gay anymore. At any given moment we would go into the independent unit and have sex before going back next-door with huge smiles on our faces.

After a few weeks of being with Tina, I felt I could trust her with anything. There were things I was desperate to tell her and I wanted to get them off my chest, as I felt I was keeping them from her. That was the first of many wrong decisions I was to make.

It was a very wrong one.

"I'm in love with you," I whispered into her ear.

"And I'm in love with you, too," she whispered back.

My time with Tina was always so good. The hours and days would fly past in no time at all.

One Friday evening, when most of the other kids had gone home on week-end leave, we had the living room to ourselves. Miss Shrill was on duty that night and, as she loved to chain smoke in the office, we were left alone to relax and watch television, cuddled up on the sofa. We both knew the sound of the office door when it opened and we always had just enough time to sit upright at opposite ends before ever being caught. As we were watching a film, I had the sudden urge to tell Tina about some of my past.

"There's some stuff I want to tell you," I said, as I held her close to me.

"What stuff?" she asked.

"Stuff from my past" I answered.

"You look like you're going to cry, Leon. What is it? You can tell me anything. You know that," she said gently.

I knew the time was now or never. I'd wanted to tell her for a while, but something inside stopped me from doing so. We were alone and I had the perfect opportunity. I told her all about the horror stories from my childhood. All she could do was cry.

"Why didn't you run away?" she sniffled.

"Well, that's what I want to tell you," I answered.

"I don't understand," she said, with a look of confusion on her face.

A strong sense of nausea came over me as I spilled the secrets about the events that had happened in London.

"I was raped," I cried.

"WHAT!" she screamed.

"I was raped over and over," I spluttered out amongst the tears.

"Who by?" she said, still in floods of tears.

Once I'd let the words spill out of my mouth, I knew there was no going back. I had to get this out in the open. I felt so dirty for holding it all in.

"By three different men," I answered.

"MEN!" she screamed.

I had known that it would come as a huge shock to her, but I hadn't been sure how she would react.

"Yes," I said as I stared at a blank spot on the living room carpet. Just then she stood up and ran from the room and up the stairs, crying all the way. I had thought that I was doing the right thing when I was saying it, but now that it was out, I felt even dirtier. Her reaction had thrown me sideways. It was as if she blamed me for what I'd let the men do to me. I couldn't believe that, only ten minutes ago, I was the happiest I'd ever been in my entire life and now, it was all caving in around me with such speed and such force.

"Tina!" I screamed, as I ran up the stairs after her.

"Go away!" she screamed, at the top of her voice.

My heart was thumping as the blood rushed to my head like a tidal wave. I was in complete despair. I had kept that secret to myself for so long, even though I'd wanted to scream out to the world many times over that I'd been abused. What was I going to do now? What was going to make this all right? Just now, nothing was going to make it all right.

With all the screaming coming from the upstairs Miss Shrill had come to investigate.

"What the hell is going on?" she demanded.

"Piss off!" I shouted, as I ran for the stairs.

I didn't know where to run. My mind was black with the poisonous fog of those memories.

The poison that I'd kept under control for over two months now. As soon as the cloud re-appeared in my mind, I knew I was in trouble. I didn't want to run away. I just wanted Tina to make everything all right; but she couldn't. It was too much for her to take in.

After sitting, huddled in the corner of the study-room, rocking backwards and forwards for what felt like an eternity, Miss Shrill appeared round the door.

"Tina has told me that you've been sleeping together," she said coldly.

I didn't care what she said. My life was already over now. Yet, what she did say next will haunt me for the rest of my life.

"You've slept with her after sleeping with men," she said with no emotion.

"I WAS RAPED!" I screamed.

"You were raped and never told anyone?" she said with disbelief.

"I was scared," I cried.

"Well that makes Tina's situation worse," she said.

"What?" I asked blankly.

"It is a horrible thing that happened to you, Leon, and we will get you someone to talk to. I can't believe you told no-one about this, and then to sleep with this Tina without a second thought to hers or your health!

What were you thinking? We must act quickly for the other side of things," she went on to explain.

"The other side……?" I asked, still confused by what she meant.

"You could have given her AIDS. You will both have to go through the trauma of finding out now," she explained.

"What's AIDS?" I asked.

"It's what men catch when they sleep with other men," she answered coldly.

"I don't know what you mean," I said.

"I don't have time to go into that right now. I need to go and calm down a very frightened girl upstairs," she said, turning away.

I slumped to the floor, in tears, as visions came into my head of the disturbing advert, on the television, that I'd seen years earlier, where the headstone read: 'Don't die of ignorance. Don't die of AIDS'.

What did she mean? Was I going to die?

Before I knew it, the home was swarming with Police and Social workers. I was told that I could be arrested for having under-age sex. Statement after statement was taken from me. I had to re-live every moment and every bit of pain that I had endured in London and Liverpool: places and names, graphic descriptions of what had gone on during my time away. I was told that I would have to go for blood tests to see if I had AIDS. The social workers explained to me the possible implications of having that disease: death.

I had been raped and used as a sex toy by men and my first chance of having a normal happy life had also just been stolen from me. I'd been right all along. I was put on this earth for one purpose and one purpose alone: to suffer.

The interviews went on for over three hours and, although the on-duty social workers were sympathetic, I couldn't help but feel that I was being blamed for putting Tina's life at risk and that my rape was of less importance.

Tina was taken away that very night and placed with a foster family. I never even had the chance to say goodbye. I didn't know if I would ever be allowed to see her again.

I had to do something and I had to do it fast. Whether I had the disease or not was completely irrelevant at that point because, the one thing I could never forgive myself for, was if I had passed a death sentence on to Tina. I was going to die if the blood test came back positive. During the cross-examination they hadn't even bothered to ask if Tina and I had used protection. If they had, it would have been obvious that there was no way she could have the disease, even if I did. We had used protection to stop her falling pregnant; I didn't realise at the time that I was also, perhaps, going to save her life.

I lay in my bedroom, staring at the ceiling, desperate to know what to do next. My heart was well and truly broken. I couldn't live with the thought of having hurt Tina. I didn't want to hang around long enough to know the outcome of any tests that would have to be taken.

As if in auto-pilot, I sneaked down the stairs and slipped out of the back door to make my way to the Mace shop at the end of Westline Road. I knew what I was going to buy. It had taken me only a few minutes to decide. I looked old enough to buy alcohol and had enough money for a half bottle of Vodka. That would do the trick, I thought to myself. That wasn't all I was after, though. I would buy two bottles of Paracetamol with the Vodka. It was my only option.

It was my only way out.

After wiping away my tears, I walked in to the shop with my head held high. I couldn't risk arousing any suspicion.

"Just these and a half bottle of Vodka please," I said, with confidence. It worked. I had my future right here in a small Mace carrier bag. I wandered back to the home and sneaked back up to my bedroom. Within minutes, I was guzzling handfuls of Paracetamol and washing them down with the vodka, retching as they went down.

This was it: my final moments on this earth. It was destiny. That's how my real Dad had done it and I was just repeating history, the way it was meant. I was going to be with my dad: my real dad.

As I slip into an unconscious state I see my dad. He is holding his hand out to me, reaching for me to be with him. He is beautiful. More beautiful than in the photograph I'd already seen. He is my guardian angel who has come to help me cross to a more peaceful world: a world with no pain, no suffering, no hurt and no poison.

"I love you, Dad," I whisper.

"I love you, too, my beautiful son," he says, with such love in his voice.

I've waited all my life for this one moment: this one precious moment of love. All the people who had come and gone in my short existence were all trapped in the world of life.

No more pain.

No more hurt.

My dad loves me. My dad has come for me.

I'm no longer alone.

Blackout.

Lights flash through my eyelids. I'm scared and I'm confused.

"DADDY!" I scream.

"LEON!"

"DADDY, PLEASE DON'T LEAVE ME!" I cry.

It's too late. He's gone.

What's happening?

Where am I?

"Leon. Leon. You're safe now. It's all going to be O.K.," says the stranger. I open my eyes. The brightness stings my eyes. I'm in a hospital.

"It's not all right. I want my Dad," I cry.

"Your dad's not here, Leon. But we are. We are here for you now," my auntie Imogen assured me, through floods of tears.

I'd been found unconscious in my bedroom when Miss Shrill had come to check that I was all right. Apparently, she had felt guilty about the way she had dealt with the drama that had unfolded earlier that evening. Once she seen the empty bottles scattered around my bed she had phoned 999 for an ambulance. My auntie had also been informed. I off-loaded fifteen years' worth of baggage that night. For the first time in my life I felt lighter and not burdened down with life's misery. For the first time in my life, my heart had emotion and wasn't just a wasting muscle inside my frame. I felt like some of my fight and spirit was rushing back through my body, like a breath of fresh air in a smoke-filled room, while I lay in that hospital bed. Talking to her, gave me such strength and such courage. Her eyes bulged with anger as I told her of my childhood horrors.

"I'm so sorry, Leon. I never knew," she whispered, with tears in her eyes.

"I just want to be loved. Is that so wrong?" I whimpered.

"We love you!" she cried.

"You do?" Tears were in full flow as self-doubt mixed with relief.

"Of course we do! Don't EVER feel alone, Leon," she cried.

I'd waited my lifetime to hear those words. They echoed around my mind, heart, body and soul. Breathing life into what I thought had died.

That should bring a close to this story.

But it doesn't. It is only the end of a chapter.

That night, spent with my aunt close by my side, was merely a gift from God.

It was merely a pit-stop to regain my strength for what was, yet, to come.

Blackout.